TOLKIEN

AND THE

PERIL of WAR

ROBERT S. BLACKHAM

The
History
Press

Title page: John Ronald Reuel Tolkien, who preferred to be called Ronald, in his army uniform.

First published 2011

The History Press
The Mill, Brimscombe Port,
Stroud, Gloucestershire, GL5 2QG
www.thehistorypress.co.uk

British Library Cataloguing in Publication Data.
A catalogue record for this book is available from the British Library.

ISBN 978 0 7524 5780 2

Typesetting and origination by The History Press
Printed in Great Britain

Contents

Acknowledgements

his book could not have been written without the help of a number of other books; here are the most thumbed and, in some cases, the most falling apart: *J.R.R. Tolkien: A Biography* by Humphrey Carpenter; *The Complete Guide to Middle-Earth* by Robert Foster; *Tolkien and the Great War* by John Garth; *The J.R.R. Tolkien Companion and Guide* by Christina Scull & Wayne G. Hammond; *Birmingham Pals* by Terry Carter; *The Somme: Death of a Generation* by John Harris; many of J.R.R. Tolkien's published works and books on the First World War left to me by my late father.

I would also like to thank the following people: the staff at The History Press past and present for helping me to get this book published; all the people who have generously contributed pictures and maps for the book; Chris Upton for his 1992 Tolkien Discovery Trail guide that got me started on writing about Tolkien; the Moseley Bog Volunteers and the Shire Country Park Rangers; the staff at Selly Manor Museum, who have put up with me going on about Tolkien for years, and Alison Houghton who introduced me to buying postcards on eBay; all the members of the Three Farthing Stone Smial at Moreton in Marsh; Kirsty Nicol and Martin Brown from No Man's Land for their help with the archaeology from the Western Front and Brocton Camp; the Tolkien Society for their help and support over the years, and all the members I have talked to about this subject; and finally I would like to thank my family, for all their support and help.

The Tolkien Society

he Tolkien Society (founded by Vera Chapman in 1969 to further interest in the life and works of J.R.R. Tolkien, CBE, the author of *The Hobbit*, *The Lord of the Rings* and other works of fiction and philological study) is proud to have Robert as a member and a work such as this adding to the scholarship on our favourite author.

Based in the UK and registered as an independent, non-profit-making charity, the Society boasts an international membership in over forty countries. The Society helps to bring together those with like minds, both formally and informally, with gatherings locally or nationally throughout the year. Recently we have been involved in weekend events in May, based at Sarehole Mill and the setting up of the Shire Country Park, and we are continuing to work with other groups in the area on Tolkien-related projects.

Our three main events at a national level are: the Annual General Meeting and Dinner, held in the spring in a different town or city in the UK each year; the Seminar, which takes place in the summer and presents a programme of talks on a Tolkien-related subject; and Oxonmoot, held over a weekend in September in an Oxford College, with a range of activities such as talks, discussions, slide-shows and a costume party.

The Society produces two publications: the bulletin, *Amon Hen*, appears six times a year, with Tolkien-related reviews, news, letters, artwork and articles, both humorous and serious; the annual journal, *Mallorn*, is more serious in nature, with longer critical articles, reviews and essays.

Within the Society there are local groups spread throughout Britain and the world called 'Smials' (after hobbit homes). Here, both members and non-members can gather to discuss Tolkien's works, as well as other writers and topics. The formality and seriousness of meetings varies depending on the members. In addition to these there are also Special Interest Groups, covering topics such as collecting, biography and Tolkien's languages. For

Young Members there is an active group, 'Entings', which has its own section in the Society bulletin.

The Society has a website which provides members and non-members with general information about itself and the world of Tolkien: http://www.tolkiensociety.org/.

The Tolkien Society
Hon. Pres.: the late Professor J.R.R. Tolkien, CBE *In Perpetuo*
Hon. Vice Pres.: Priscilla Tolkien
Founded in 1969 by Vera Chapman
Registered Charity No. 273809

Introduction

his book has been a long time in the making, with many twists and turns along the way. I first started looking into Tolkien's life and works many years ago, in mine and Tolkien's childhood haunts of the Cole Valley and Sarehole Mill. While writing *Tolkien's Oxford*, I had to write a linking chapter – *Marriage, War and Return to Oxford* – to get the book through the First World War. After about four months of working on the chapter I had obtained a large quantity of books, pictures and maps to do with the Battle of the Somme. Then the penny dropped, here was another book about Tolkien, so I packed all that material away and finished *Tolkien's Oxford*. The other thing I can remember from that time was being at Wayland's Smithy on a summer's day; my eyes were drawn to a rusting barbed-wire fence and I wondered what survivors of the war thought when they saw fences like this – were their minds taken back to the dark days in the trenches?

The First World War was a pivotal point for Tolkien's generation. The time before the war was thought of as a golden-age; afterwards the world was made up of survivors, most of whom had lost friends and relations during the conflict, and much of the old world had gone forever. Tolkien started the war as a student in Oxford and finished the war as a married man with a wife and a child; throughout this period he was writing. However, he did say in the 1960s that in the squalor and shabbiness of the trenches he was not doing very much writing at all, so most of his writing must have been done on leave, in camp or in hospital.

During the war he was still in contact with his school friends from the Tea Club, Barrovian Society, 'TCBS'. They met as a group, or sometimes as just a couple of friends, and wrote and exchanged their current works and writings, giving support and literary criticism to one another. I have only touched briefly on this part of Tolkien's life as it has been covered in greater detail by other books; I have chosen instead to focus more on the actual war and on events in Tolkien's life during those years.

His period of active service during the Battle of the Somme can only be summed up as intense, and the experience most likely stayed with him for the rest of his life. In my opinion, it re-emerged in his writing years later. This was where the first seeds of Mordor were sown in Tolkien's mind, as is shown from a letter written in 1977 to *The Listener* by Graham Tayar – also a student of King Edward's School in Birmingham. Tayar writes that Tolkien 'once told me that the physical setting [of Mordor] derived directly from the trenches of World War One, the wasteland of shell-cratered battlefields where he fought in 1916'. (*The J.R.R. Tolkien Companion and Guide*, Volume 11)

Maybe to survive the brutality of trench warfare and army life, soldiers had to become a bit Orc-like. But, having said that, the courage of the men and women on both sides of the front line must have been awesome in the face of the perverted science of poison-gas and flame-throwers, and the more 'conventional' weapons of bombs, shells and bullets.

I have not been to the Somme battlefield, but I have been to the battlefield at Loos in Northern France where my grandfather James Ernest Morriss was killed in 1915. He has no known grave and his name is recorded on the cemetery wall along with 24,000 other soldiers. These places were built as memorials to the fallen in the war, to give closure to their friends and relatives. I must admit that I found the place painful, seeing such a waste of human life. His wife, my grandmother, Elizabeth Ann Morriss, also died in the war but on the home front; in a strange way this book about Tolkien is dedicated to my lost grandparents. They were small people who were swept up by world events – this is one of the main themes running through Tolkien's *The Lord of the Rings*, and maybe the First World War did play a part in the creation of Tolkien's Middle-earth.

The First World War still affects the world we live in today. Though the last survivors of the war have left the stage, it is still important that we remember the sacrifice that was made by their generation in our recent past.

1

Prelude to War

he roots of what today we call the First World War are many and various, but the immediate events that led to the outbreak of hostilities started on 28 June 1914, with the assassination of Archduke Franz Ferdinand and his wife in Bosnia. The Archduke at the time was wearing a bullet-proof vest, but was shot through the neck. He was killed by a Serbian nationalist student, Gavrilo Princip, a member of the Black Hand group in Sarajevo, where the Archduke had gone to inspect Austro-Hungarian troops on Bosnia's national day. Bosnia had been annexed from Turkey and taken into the Austro-Hungarian Empire, which the Archduke was the heir to, and this was strongly resented by Serbia.

The Archduke and his wife were in an open-top car and were leaving Sarajevo when their driver took a wrong turn; the car had stopped and was reversing when Gavrilo Princip, who was walking by, came across the car and shot them. The Austrian Government blamed the Serbian Government for the killing and, on 28 July 1914, declared war on Serbia. Russia was allied with Serbia, but the German Government did not think that Russia would mobilise their armed forces and offered support to the Austrian Government. However, the Russians did mobilise, and called on their alliance with France to mobilise their armed forces, and so Germany declared war on Russia on 1 August 1914.

> 10-25PM.REUTERS TEL. GERMANY DECLARS
> WAR ON RUSSIA. ST PETERSBURG.AUG.1
> T GERMAN AMBASSADOR IN T NAME O HIS
> GOVT HANDED TO T FOREIGN MINISTRY A
> DECLARATION O WAR AT 7-30 THIS
> EVENING.REUTER.10-27

Photograph of the fateful message declaring war, which came over the tape machine to a newspaper office on 1 August 1914. The single T stands for 'the' in the message.

Germany declared war on France on 3 August 1914 and the German Army, using the Schlieffen Plan, invaded Belgium, which was neutral. The British sent an ultimatum to the Germans to withdraw from Belgium – which they did not do – and so Britain declared war on Germany on 4 August 1914. The First World War was up and running.

It just goes to show what a wrong turn in a car can lead to!

2

Tolkien's Pre-War Years

 olkien's military training had started in his schooldays at King Edward's School in Birmingham, where he was a member of the Officers' Training Corps. He had then gone to Exeter College, Oxford, in 1911 to study Classics, but had later changed to English Language. At college he had joined the King Edward's Horse regiment, which recruited from British residents born overseas – he had been born in southern Africa in 1892. He remained in the regiment till the January of 1913, when he was discharged at his own request. In the summer of 1912 he had been on a two-week camp with the regiment near Folkestone in Kent, and the weather had been very wet and windy. A life under canvas in poor weather may not have been to Ronald's liking, and this could have been the reason he left the regiment. Alternatively, the reason could have been his reunion with his teenage sweetheart, Edith Mary Bratt.

He had first met Edith at the age of sixteen when living in Duchess Road, Edgbaston in Birmingham; they were both orphans and were lodging in the same house.

Children playing in Duchess Road, Edgbaston, in the early twentieth century.

He had been forbidden from meeting, talking to, or corresponding with Edith by his guardian Father Francis Morgan, from the Oratory Church in Edgbaston, who controlled some of the money that Ronald required for his education at Exeter College. However, on his twenty-first birthday on 3 January 1913, Ronald came of age and hence took charge of his own finances.

In the early hours of 3 January, when they had been apart for almost three long years, Ronald wrote to Edith: 'How long will it be before we can be joined together before God and the world?' (*J.R.R. Tolkien: A Biography*, Humphrey Carpenter). Edith wrote back to Ronald, but it was not good news as she was engaged to be married to George Field, who she said was a good man and was the brother of Molly, a school friend. Edith did imply in her letter to Ronald that she was worried about being 'left on the shelf', as she was twenty-four at the time, and also thought that he may have forgotten her during his three years at Exeter College, but stated that because Ronald had written to her these matters might change. Ronald arranged to visit Edith in Cheltenham on 8 January and, after spending the day together, Edith decided to marry Ronald.

Edith and her cousin Jennie Grove moved into rooms in Warwick, where Edith took instruction from Father Murphy in the Catholic faith as Tolkien was a Catholic. She became a Roman Catholic in January 1914.

The nave of the new Oratory Church in Edgbaston, built between 1903 and 1906, with its tunnel-vaulted ceiling in chestnut-wood, which was decorated in1959.

3
Tolkien and the Early War Years

n August 1914, Ronald Tolkien was on vacation from Exeter College. The war was to change his life in many ways over the next few years, as it was for millions of people throughout the world.

In late August, Tolkien was staying in Warwick to spend time with Edith; they had become formally engaged earlier in the year. In September he visited Phoenix Farm in Gedling, Nottinghamshire, which was run by his Aunt Jane Neave and her farming partner Ellen Brookes-Smith. Tolkien's younger brother Hilary was also living and working at the farm. His Aunt Jane was the younger sister of his mother Mabel, and was a powerful guiding force for both of the Tolkien brothers; they were in contact with her until her death in 1963. Aunt Jane was widowed in 1909 by the death of her husband Edwin Neave, and had struck out into the man's world of farming – which it must be said was no mean feat at a time when women had very few rights within society. Jane had purchased Church Farm – later to be renamed Phoenix Farm – by auction in Nottingham in March 1911, and then bought Manor Farm in July 1911. I strongly suspect that she chose the name Phoenix Farm to symbolise that she was making a new start after her husband's death.

Jane was to play a part in Ronald's development of Middle-earth, and it is said that her wisdom and powerful personality possibly helped Tolkien to form the character of Gandalf in the books. However, there are also a number of strong female characters featured in *The Lord of the Rings*, such as Lady Éowyn and Lady Galadriel, who could have been based on Jane, or even on Tolkien's mother, Mabel Tolkien. Aunt Jane's later farm in Dormston, Worcestershire, which was called Bag End, was to emerge as the home of Bilbo and Frodo in *The Hobbit* and *The Lord of the Rings* years later.

During Ronald's stay at Phoenix Farm, he wrote the first draft of the poem 'The Voyage of Eärendil the Evening Star'. The Evening Star is a common name for Venus, which appears in the western sky after sunset. Tolkien had come across the name Eärendil in a group of Anglo-Saxon poems (known as a Crist), with two lines particularly inspiring him: *eala earendel engla beorhtast* ('Hail Earendel, brightest of angels') and *ofer middangeard monnum ended* ('sent over Middle-earth to men').

All Hallows Church, Gedling, which stood a short distance from Church Farm (later renamed Phoenix Farm by Jane Neave). The fine 89ft tower and 91ft spire were built in the fourteenth century, becoming major landmarks in the area as they soar towards the heavens.

Gedling railway station. Ronald and Hilary would have used this station when they travelled to Phoenix Farm in Gedling.

On 11 October 1914, Ronald returned to Oxford for the start of the Michaelmas term. He was not going to 'join up' as many young men of his age were, but was going to carry on with his studies at Exeter College. He was no longer living at Exeter College but had rooms in St John Street, a short distance from the college. Ronald joined the Officers' Training Corps and started drilling in the University Parks from 9 a.m. to 10 a.m. on Monday, Wednesday, Friday and Saturday, in all weathers. He was also attending lectures or classes on signalling and map reading. He was most likely drawing his rifle for drilling from the Territorial Headquarters on Cross Road, off South Park Road on the town side of the University Parks. The rifles would have been cleaned and oiled after each drilling session to keep them in good working order.

Ronald had changed his college course in 1913 from Classics to English and, in June 1915, he was to take his examination for the Honour School of English Language and Literature. His first exam was on 10 June at the Sheldonian Theatre on Broad Street; the exams started at 9.30 a.m. and 2 p.m. and each lasted three hours. He did further exams on the 11th, 12th, 14th and 15th of June.

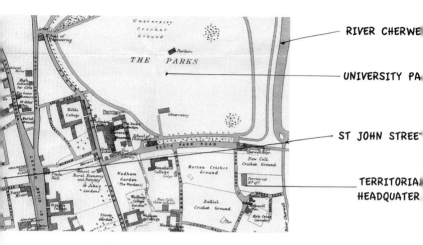

RIVER CHERWE

UNIVERSITY PA

ST JOHN STREE

TERRITORIA
HEADQUATER

University Parks was a short walk for Tolkien from his rooms in St John Street.

Exeter College front quadrangle, where signalling training was given to the college students in the Oxford University Officers' Training Corps in 1914. On the right of the picture is the college chapel, which was designed by George Gilbert-Scott and is based on Sainte Chapelle in Paris. The spire, or flèche, is a significant landmark on the Oxford skyline.

Balliol College was one of the many colleges in Oxford that formed the Oxford University Officers' Training Corps. It was one of twenty-three such units established in 1908 by Royal Warrant. The Officers' Training Corps was established to provide well-trained officers for the reserve and regular army.

University Parks, viewed across the pool in the north-east corner of the park.

The Sheldonian Theatre viewed from the rear of the Clarendon; here, in June 1915, Tolkien sat his Examination for the Honour School of English Language and Literature.

The interior of the Sheldonian Theatre.

Having completed his exams on 28 June 1915, Ronald applied for a temporary commission in the army for the period of the war; a couple of days after this he was given a grant of £50 to purchase his uniform and kit. To put the military grant into context, when he won his scholarship to Exeter College in December 1910, his yearly grant was £60, so the army grant was quite a large sum of money.

Tolkien's school friend and fellow member of the TCBS, Geoffrey Smith, wrote to Ronald in June 1915 to advise him on the kit he would need to purchase for his army service.

Smith recommended the Birmingham outfitter called Allports (located at 21-23 Colmore Row in the city centre) for uniforms, and stated that his had not shown any signs of wear since he had purchased it. Tolkien would need to buy a sleeping bag, bed, cork mattress, down pillow, rugs, bath and washstand, blankets, soap-box, hooks for tent-poles, ground sheet (which Smith considered optional) and a kitbag. One important item that Tolkien would also require was a tin box to keep his underwear in.

Tolkien also needed a Sam Browne belt. The belt was usually made from leather; it consisted of a wide belt around the waist with a narrower belt going diagonally over the right shoulder. Smith recommended that the belt should have D rings on the back, on which to hang such items as a mackintosh, haversack and a water-bottle when going on marches. Strangely, Smith was not too worried whether or not Tolkien could obtain a water-bottle, as he had lost his. However, a lack of clean drinking water was a big problem for troops fighting in the trenches, as Tolkien was perhaps to find out.

> The water was cool but not icy, and it had an unpleasant taste, at once bitter and oily, or so they would have said at home. Here it seemed beyond all praise, and beyond fear or prudence. They drank their fill, and Sam replenished his water-bottle.
>
> (*The Return of the King*, The Land of Shadow, J.R.R. Tolkien)

Smith also recommended the Birmingham Household Supply Association at 150-8 Corporation Street in Birmingham city centre for other, household, items that Tolkien might require for his kit. Smith was rather uncertain about where Tolkien should go to buy his boots. But he was very clear about where Tolkien should go to buy his wristwatch, and this was Henry Greaves in New Street, Birmingham city centre. Before the war, wristwatches had been worn by ladies, and men would have had pocket-watches – but it took time to get your watch out of your pocket and seconds really counted in this war, where timing was critical.

Edwardian actress and singer Phyllis Dare proudly wearing her wristwatch.

Smith had been at Corpus Christi College, Oxford at the same time that Ronald was at Exeter College, and they were great friends. Smith had also joined Oxford University Officers' Training Corps in October 1914, but in December 1914 he had applied for a commission in the army and had joined the 19th Lancashire Fusiliers; he went to France in November 1915.

On 3 July 1915, Tolkien was awarded a First Class Honours Degree and this was announced in *The Times* newspaper on the same day. Also in July, he visited Edith in Warwick, and relatives in Moseley and Barnt Green.

An officer's trench watch from 1916 with a solid silver case, and radium painted numbers and hands so the time could be read in the dark. This would have cost around 40 shillings at the time. It looks a bit like a pocket watch that has had the chain removed and heavy-duty lugs fitted to the case to attach the watch to its strap. It is reading a few seconds before 7.30 a.m., the fateful time when the whistles blew and the first wave of troops went over the top on 1 July 1916 at the Somme. (Courtesy of Joel Clarke)

On 9 July, Tolkien's commission as a temporary second lieutenant was issued by the War Office, to take effect from 15 July. He was to be in the infantry; this was announced in *The Times* on 17 July. So his name had been mentioned in *The Times* twice in the month of July for two very different reasons!

On 19 July he went to Bedford to start his officer training.

4

Ꮒilary Tolkien

ilary Tolkien volunteered for the army in the early September of 1914. At the time, there was a wave of patriotic fervour to 'join up' passing through Britain and the Empire. It was said at the time that the war would be over by Christmas.

Hilary joined the 3rd Birmingham Battalion and their start-up was a bit low key – they were given their bus fare and told to report to Spring Hill College, Wake Green Road, or, as Hilary would have known it from his childhood, the Pine Dell Hydropathic Establishment and Moseley Botanical Gardens. The 1st and 2nd Birmingham Battalions' send-off was a much grander affair; they paraded through Birmingham to New Street station, from where they departed for training camps.

Hilary had lived further down the Wake Green Road with his mother and Ronald at 5 Gracewell Cottages in the 1890s, and had visited the buildings in 1897 to attend a garden party to celebrate Queen Victoria's jubilee. He was returning to his and Ronald's childhood haunts in much-changed

The drums and bugles of the Royal Warwickshire Regiment, 16th (service) battalion (3rd Birmingham) band at Moseley Barracks. Hilary Tolkien is standing on the back row, second in from the left-hand side, with a moustache. (Courtesy of Terry Carter)

16th (Service) Battalion Royal Warwickshire Regiment.

DRUMS.

Roll No.	Rank and Name.	Roll No.	Rank and Name.
334	Sergeant GRIGG, I. F.	366	Drummer HEWITT, F.
539	Corporal CLARKE, S. S.	302	„ BLOUNT, W.
501	L.-Corpl. ASBURY, C.	765	„ BAKER, A.
843	„ SHORT, H.	1168	„ CASTLE, J.
953	„ NICHOLLS, H.	297	„ COHEN, H.
926	„ WATSON, O. E.	93	„ STONE, W.
267	Drummer BUNCE, C. E.	1328	„ WILLIAMS, A. G.
837	„ GOODE, H.	771	„ BAKER, S. G.
984	„ PARTRIDGE, T. H.	1095	„ STRONG, W. H.
1247	„ RIVERS, J.	1020	„ TOLKIEN, H. A. R.
362	„ HOPKINS, H.	90	„ SAUNDERS, W.
729	„ WILLIAMS, S. F.	894	„ ROBINSON, J.
795	„ CROSS, H.	767	„ BILL, N. H.
918	„ JEFFS, C. H.	1079	„ BURTON, A.
1009	„ STARBUCK, F.	831	„ GIBBS, H. G.
369	„ IRELAND, G. C.	1169	„ CASTLE, W. E.
779	„ BENTLEY, F. E.	639	„ MAYBURY, T. W.
677	„ PAYNTING, H. M.		

Also on the Photograph : Major A. B. LOVEKIN, Captain A. HARDY-SMITH, Captain F. A. PARRY, and Sergt.-Major P. S. MORGAN.

The following were not present when the Photograph was taken :—

1291	Drummer WARNER, A.	266	Drummer BLAYMIRES, W. J.
1231	„ GIBBS, H.	700	„ STEEL, W. H.
828	„ FAULKES, L.	783	„ WATSON, B.
1251	„ HAZLETON, L.	669	„ PECK, W. R.
1285	„ EWINS, W.	808	„ DOWNEY, A. T.
833	„ GREATREX, W.		

A list of the soldiers in the adjacent photograph. Hilary Tolkien is recorded as being present and his name is shown in the right-hand column, ten places down from the top. (Courtesy of Terry Carter)

circumstances, and memories of his dead mother and his childhood probably stirred in his mind.

The military took over the college buildings in the middle of September 1914 and renamed it Moseley Barracks; it had lain empty since 1900. Hilary was to become a drummer and bugler in the battalion's band; this also meant that he was a stretcher-bearer in the battalion, as was army practice at the time. At Moseley Barracks, Hilary would have drilled, undertaken weapon handling and received rudimentary first-aid training. Stretcher-bearers usually worked in pairs to recover first the wounded soldiers from the battlefield and then the bodies of the dead troops; they would 'scoop and run'. When the ground was very muddy, they would have to work in teams of four to recover the wounded and dead. The wounded would be carried back to field dressing stations, which were just behind the front line trenches in the reserve trenches, to have their wounds cleaned and dressed. They were then taken back to the field hospitals for emergency treatment.

Some of the 3rd Birmingham Battalion band at Moseley Barracks. Hilary is at the back of the picture on the left-hand side. (Courtesy of Terry Carter)

Some of the soldiers of the 3rd Birmingham Battalion outside the main entrance to Moseley Barracks. This building was to become Moseley School and is now Spring Hill College, returning to the name it originally had when the college was built. (Courtesy of Terry Carter)

The tented camp of the 3rd Birmingham Battalion on Malvern Common, Worcestershire, in April 1915. (Courtesy of Terry Carter)

Stretcher-bearer training at the camp on Malvern Common, Worcestershire, in 1915. Note the bearers, a two-man team, are taking most of the weight of their patient via slings over their shoulders. (Courtesy of Terry Carter)

The 3rd Birmingham Battalion band at Malvern Common, Worcestershire in 1915. It looks as though the battalion has visitors, as a few ladies can be seen on the grass beside the band – most likely the wives and mothers of the soldiers. Hilary Tolkien can be seen in the line on the right-hand side, fourth back from the front. (Courtesy of Terry Carter)

All soldiers also carried their own field dressing kit, so they could attempt to treat their own wounds.

In April 1915, Hilary's battalion moved to a tented camp at Malvern, Worcestershire; in June to a huge army camp in the grounds of Bolton Hall in Wensleydale, Yorkshire; and then in late July to a camp at Hornsea on the North Sea coast. In August, the battalion moved to Codford St Mary on Salisbury Plain, and on 21 November 1915 they departed from Folkestone for Boulogne in France.

During Hilary's time in the army, Edith Bratt – who at the start of the war was only engaged to Ronald (though later became his wife) – was listed as his next of kin. It must have seemed a long time since their teenage years at Duchess Road in Edgbaston; and how much the world had changed.

Hilary saw active service on the Western Front and in northern Italy throughout the war, and was slightly wounded on a number of occasions. As a stretcher-bearer, he would have seen the horrors of war many, many times while doing his duties. He returned home to the West Midlands on 17 February 1919, which was his twenty-fifth birthday.

5

Bedford

n Bedford, Ronald Tolkien was billeted in a house with six other training officers; lower ranks were crammed in, with many dozens to a house. His training was undertaken on De Pary's Avenue, where he was taught how to drill a platoon, and had lectures in military custom and practice. A likely candidate for the location where he was trained is Bedford School. He grew a moustache, most likely to make himself look older than he was.

With a group of fellow officers he bought a motorbike; this would enable him to travel to Warwick to see Edith when he got a weekend pass, a round trip of about 100 miles. He finished his training in August and was posted to Whittington Heath Barracks in Staffordshire to join his battalion.

Bunyan Statue, Bedford.

There is a fine statue of John Bunyan standing at the end of De Pary's Avenue. Bunyan was born in what is now Bedford on 28 November 1628; the statue may have reminded Tolkien of his days, only a short while before, of studying English Language and Literature back in Oxford.

Religious panels from the base of the John Bunyan statue and the bronze door in Bedford. Bunyan wrote *Pilgrim's Progress* while serving twelve years' imprisonment in Bedford Gaol.

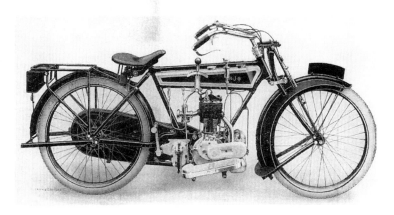

Tolkien and a group of fellow officers purchased an AJS motorbike jointly when he was training in Bedford. This is a typical AJS model from the period. (Courtesy of the Vintage Motor Cycle Club)

6

Staffordshire

olkien moved to Whittington Barracks just outside Lichfield in Staffordshire. The barracks had been built in the late 1870s and opened in 1880. The barracks is still in use today, and the parade ground where Tolkien would have drilled his men is there too – but most of the buildings he would have known are long gone. The site is used today by the Defence Medical Services. Tolkien would have been under canvas in a bell tent, most likely camped on the old Whittington racecourse next to the barracks (*see* map on p.32). He was serving with the 13th Battalion of the Lancashire Fusiliers, who had been raised in Hull in

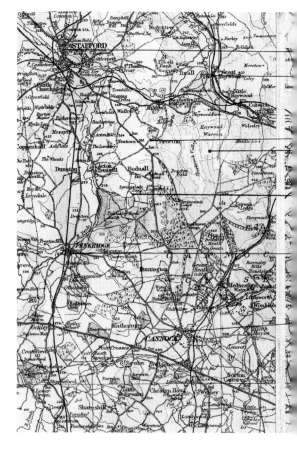

Map of Cannock Chase and part of Staffordshire. The map dates from the 1920s – which is after Brocton and Rugeley Camps had been removed from the landscape – but a faint echo of the camps can still be perceived on the map. The roads built on the Chase to serve the camps can still be seen.

December 1914. The battalion was used to replenish battalions at the front, making good their losses and bringing them back to full strength. Tolkien, however, would not be going to war with his platoon of some sixty men.

Tolkien had to prepare his men for war; they had been drawn from a wide social background and he came to the conclusion that for the last few years he had been living in an 'ivory tower'. Camp life was very bureaucratic, which he disliked.

In mid-October, Tolkien and his battalion moved to the – still under construction – camp at Rugeley, on Cannock Chase in Staffordshire.

At the start of the war in 1914 there were barracks in Britain for around 175,000 men, but by December 1914 over a million men had enlisted, and housing them had become a major problem. Plans were put in action to build hutted camps to house the troops; by the summer of 1915 there were places for 850,000 troops within hutted camps. This was a major undertaking carried out at great speed, as the camps not only had huts but roads, railway

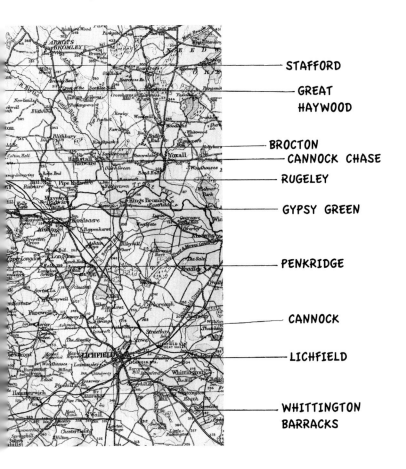

STAFFORD

GREAT
HAYWOOD

BROCTON
CANNOCK CHASE
RUGELEY

GYPSY GREEN

PENKRIDGE

CANNOCK

LICHFIELD

WHITTINGTON
BARRACKS

Soldiers on guard duty outside a military barracks in early 1916.

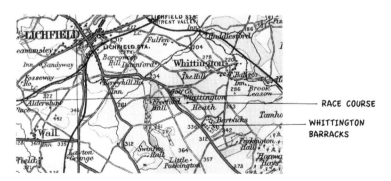

RACE COURSE

WHITTINGTON
BARRACKS

Map of the Lichfield area of Staffordshire. Whittington Barracks can be seen in the right-hand lower corner of the map, with the old racecourse just above it.

Rugeley Camp on Cannock Chase. Evidence of construction work can be seen in front of the complete lines of huts adjacent to the curving railway track.

lines, water supplies, sewerage systems and even power stations. Also, building the huts would have required the importation of tens of thousands of tons of timber, as Britain at the time had very little woodland. In 1919, the Forestry Commission was set up to plant and grow trees; this was to ensure that Britain would never be short of timber again. Echoes of the wartime shortage of timber can be seen today in the plantations of conifer trees on Cannock Chase. The name Cannock, incidentally, comes from the combination of two Old English words, 'Cann' meaning powerful and 'Aic' meaning oak.

The sites of the two camps on Cannock Chase were chosen for their central location and access to main line railways. The area had been used for military training in the past and the land was not suitable for agriculture. The land was owned by Lord Lichfield, who gave his permission for its use.

The two camps were Brocton Camp (a part of this camp was built on Anson's Bank, which was a short distance from the main camp) and Rugeley Camp (that also included the Penkridge Bank portion, separated from the main camp by Sherbrook Valley). When the two camps were completed they could house 40,000 men between them, with Brocton being the bigger of the two. They were to become small towns for the duration of the war, with hospitals, banks, post offices, YMCAs, branches of W.H. Smith, cinemas, and canteen grocery depots, which were all staffed by local people.

Once the camps were up and running they were to have a great effect on the villages, hamlets and local towns of Rugeley, Cannock and Penkridge, where the local public houses and shops did a roaring trade from soldiers who were having a couple of hours away from the camps. The mixture of fit young men – away from military discipline – and beer did lead to some local difficulties, and Cannock was made out of bounds to the troops for a period in September 1916. It is said that in the small villages of Milford and Brocton, every other house was serving tea to the off-duty soldiers and their wives and girlfriends.

Accommodation around the camps for soldiers' wives and parents was in short supply, and this drove up the cost of housing in the area. Most people, though, were only stopping for a short period before their son or husband was posted overseas. For many, this was the last time they would ever see their loved ones again.

Training for Tolkien and his platoon was a bleak affair, as the autumn turned to winter and the wind blew across the almost tree-less Chase. They learnt the skills of war, undertook drilling and physical training, and were taught shooting on the rifle ranges, how to dig zig-zag trench systems, how to survive gas attacks, and the art of signalling.

Tolkien was billeted in the Penkridge Bank section of Rugeley Camp. Camp life was not to his liking, but at least the officers' huts had several stoves in them for heating. The lower ranks had just one stove per hut. The huts were smoky due to leaky chimney pipes and the atmosphere was 'scented' by tobacco smoke, human sweat, boot polish, musty clothes drying by the stove on wet days, rifle-oil, and even beer if some of the lads had been at the pub for a couple of hours.

When Tolkien was in his billet, the background noise of the camp must have leaked through the thin walls – a cacophony of marching men, shouted orders, rifle fire from the ranges and men, and horses and machines moving along the camp roads. Perhaps Tolkien harked back to his student days of privilege back in Oxford.

Tolkien wrote to Edith Bratt on 26 November 1915 and gave her a brief outline of his day:

> The usual kind of morning standing about and freezing and then trotting to get warmer so as to freeze again. We ended up by an hour's bomb throwing with dummies. Lunch and a freezing afternoon ... now we stand in icy groups

in the open being talked at! Tea and another scramble – I fought for a place at
the stove and made a piece of toast on the end of a knife: what days!

> (*The Letters of J.R.R. Tolkien*, Letter No.3,
> Humphrey Carpenter and Christopher Tolkien)

In December, the 13th Lancashire Fusiliers moved across Cannock Chase to
Brocton Camp, and Tolkien was getting involved with the skills and craft of
becoming a signalling officer. Whether he moved to signalling as a way to
stay alive in the trenches (at the time, an officer leading a platoon on the
Western Front had a life expectancy of six weeks) or whether his natural
interest in languages and codes meant that he felt he could contribute
something to his brigade's well-being, is hard to determine. It could have
been six of one and half a dozen of the other.

On 1 December 1915, Tolkien had his first poem in print. 'Goblin Feet'
was published in *Oxford Poetry* by national publisher Sir Basil Blackwell, the
son of the founder of Blackwell's bookshop in Broad Street, Oxford. At the
time, Sir Basil was the owner of the family publishing and bookshop empire.
Many years later, Tolkien and his family were to live at 20 Northmoor Road,
which had been the home of Sir Basil. This is where Tolkien wrote *The Hobbit*
and most of *The Lord of the Rings*.

Methods used for signalling in the war were wide-ranging and diverse,
and could include the following: semaphore flags, heliograph (used to flash
Morse signals), lime-light lamps, dogs, carrier-pigeons, despatch riders,
runners, buzzers, rockets, telegraph and telephone systems and exchanges,
and, later in the war, trench wirelesses came into active service. The wireless
sets were prone to a strange form of interference – very loud crackling noises.
The noises were later discovered to have come from the planet Jupiter, being
caused by thunderstorms which can be seen from space in the form of white
spots in the atmosphere, with huge lightning discharges in the storms.

So, there was a lot for Tolkien to get his head around and good
communication was the corner-stone of warfare in winning or losing a
battle. Many of the methods of communication created light or sound
that could be seen or heard by the enemy; this made the communications
officers and men prime targets to be taken out.

In early 1916, Ronald and Edith decided to get married. Ronald could see
that his training days were coming to an end and he would soon be going
overseas, and the odds of surviving on the Western Front were looking
pretty poor. He sold his share in the AJS motorbike and went to Birmingham
to see Father Francis Morgan at the Oratory, to sort out outstanding money
matters. He was going to tell Father Francis about his plans to marry Edith,
but the ghost of Father Francis's ban on him seeing Edith in 1910 appears to

CAMP, BROCTON.

TO GREET YOU.

THERE are places in England to Brocton superior,
    In fact, it was known long ago as Siberia!
My word! it is like it,—from towns far away,—
Nothing but Khaki to make the place gay.

It's not too exciting as you may well guess,
For shops there are few and trains there are less,
But men there are plenty to cross the blue sea,
A fine lot of fellows—of course counting me!

Each man has his fairy, not always a Mary,
He thinks of her much as he sings "Tipperary,"
He marches right briskly under weight of his pack,
And dreams that "C.B." only means "coming back"!

And this is from one of them to wish you "good luck,"
He is hoping to prove he's not wanting in pluck,
Here's a handful of love from lone Cannock Chase,
From a lad who just longs for a sight of your face!

A postcard that the troops could send home from Brocton Camp. 'CB' most likely means 'confined to barracks'. The same card was sent from Rugeley Camp but the name was changed at the top of the postcard.

have put him off. He did write to him in early March 1916, however, telling him about the forthcoming wedding. Father Francis offered to marry them at the Oratory and conduct the service himself, and gave the couple his blessing. His offer had to be turned down, as the wedding was arranged to take place in Warwick later that month.

Just six days before the wedding, Ronald went to Oxford for his degree ceremony which had been delayed; it must have been a very strange experience, returning to his academic roots and comparing them to his current camp life in the army.

Soldiers walking along one of the tracks close to Brocton Camp on Cannock Chase during the First World War. The camp can just be made out in the back of the picture.

Chase Road Corner, with the Anson's Bank section of Brocton Camp in the background and a lone horse-and-cart coming along the road.

OCTON CAMP 8.

Brocton Camp, looking west across Old Acre Valley. A steamroller, most likely for road construction, is coming up the hill with a horse-and-cart overtaking it.

Brocton Camp, Cannock Chase. In the front of the picture, soldiers can be seen digging training trenches; behind them are soldiers drilling. On the right of the picture are white canvas bell tents; behind them is the camp water tower / tank. In the middle are the four chimneys for the camp power station, with rows of army huts as far as the eye can see. In *The Return of the King*, Frodo and Sam come across an army camp on their journey through Mordor that sounds similar to Brocton or Rugeley Camp.

> ... there were camps, some of tents, ordered like small towns. One of the largest of these was right below them. Barely a mile out into the plain it clustered like some huge nest of insects, with straight dreary streets of huts and long low drab buildings. About it the ground was busy with folk going to and fro ...

Troops training with fixed bayonets, crossing a freshly dug trench.

I have often wondered if Tolkien's Morse code training was to play a part in *The Lord of the Rings*. Perhaps, one night in his study in Northmoor Road, it sparked an idea when he was writing the chapter 'A Journey in the Dark' in *The Fellowship of the Ring*, when Pippin dropped the stone down the well?

> Nothing more was heard for several minutes; but then there came out of the depths faint knocks: tom-tap, tap-tom. They stopped and when the echoes had died away, they were repeated: tap-tom, tom-tap, tap-tap, and tom. They sounded disquietingly like signals of some sort; but after a while the knocking died away and was not heard again.

By using the Morse code alphabet and taking tap to be dot and tom to be dash, you can work out the first letter of a word, and this gives you a possible message.

The first message is tom-tap and tap-tom, which is dash-dot (N) and dot-dash (A).

So, the message could be Noise Above.

The second message is tap-tom, tom-tap, tap-tap and tom; this gives us dot-dash (A), dash-dot (N), dot-dot (I) and dash (T).

So, the message *could* be Alarm Noise Intruders Trouble. This is something that readers can play with, de-coding their own messages.

7

Mr and Mrs Tolkien

onald and Edith were married by Father Murphy in St Mary Immaculate Roman Catholic Church on 22 March 1916 in Warwick. They married on a Wednesday, as it was on a Wednesday that they met on 8 January 1913, when their relationship restarted back in Cheltenham. Ronald most likely wore his army uniform for the wedding ceremony, because, at the time, it was safer for young men to be seen in public in uniform; it stopped people calling them a coward and giving them white feathers. Ronald probably felt quite at home in St Mary Immaculate Church, as it is said to be very similar inside to St Aloysius' Church, where he had worshipped in Oxford during his time at Exeter College.

St Mary Immaculate Church in Warwick, built in 1859-60. The church was designed by E.W. Pugin, who was the son of A.W.N. Pugin, a leading figure in the Gothic Revival and the designer of the Palace of Westminster.

Clevedon, viewed from Salthouse Hill. This is a small seaside resort in North Somerset where Mr and Mrs Tolkien spent their honeymoon in 1916.

The Green Beach, Clevedon, with the bandstand in the background. This could well have been a scene from 1916, when Ronald and Edith were on their honeymoon. Very few men were promenading along the beach path because most of them were in military service – either overseas or in camps throughout Britain or the Empire.

The Immaculate Conception Roman Catholic Church, Clevedon. If Ronald and Edith wanted to attend mass while on their honeymoon, this would have been the place to go. (Courtesy of John Everett, of Footsteps)

After the wedding, the newlyweds travelled by train on the Great Western Railway from Warwick to Birmingham, then to Bristol, and then to Clevedon in North Somerset on the Bristol Channel coast for their week-long honeymoon. There were plenty of fine walks for the couple to take in the bays and valleys around Clevedon and, of course, they could go promenading along the pier to take their minds off the war.

During Ronald and Edith's stay in Clevedon, they went for a day trip to Cheddar Gorge; it is only six stations down a branch line through the Mendip Hills from Clevedon. The gorge and the caves at Cheddar were to be the basis for Helm's Deep and the 'glittering caves' in *The Lord of the Rings*.

> It may interest you to know that the passage was based on the caves in Cheddar Gorge and was written just after I revisited these in 1940 but was still coloured by my memory of them much earlier before they became so commercialized. I had been there during my honeymoon nearly thirty years before.
>
> (*The Letters of J.R.R. Tolkien*, Letter No.321,
> Humphrey Carpenter and Christopher Tolkien)

The Cheddar Water, or Cheddar Yeo, starts as a stream near Charterhouse on the Mendip Hills before it disappears into the limestone to reappear in Gough's Cave in the Cheddar Cave system. Gough's Cave was discovered in

Jacob's Ladder climbing out of Cheddar Gorge, with Roland Pavey's watch-tower at the top on the right-hand side of the stairs. Pavey also had Jacob's Ladder built.

Mr R.C. Gough, discoverer of the cave now named after him.

1903 and was named after its discoverer. Britain's oldest complete human skeleton was found in the cave and is estimated to be 9,000 years old. Cox's Cave was discovered in 1837 and is also named after its discoverer; it is smaller than Gough's Cave but is home to many intricate formations.

Cheddar Gorge was formed by winter snow melt water over the last 1.2 million years and the gorge is 137m (449ft) at its deepest point. One interesting feature in the gorge is a flight of 274 steps up to the top of the cliffs called Jacob's Ladder and, at the top, a wooden watch-tower which stood till 1936. The tower was built by an eccentric gentleman, Roland Pavey, and he called it his Mystic Tower. From the tower, Glastonbury Tor could be viewed. The tower was replaced in 1936 by a wrought iron tower that has forty-eight steps to the viewing platform. It is interesting to speculate, and only speculate, that Tolkien took Jacob's Ladder as the model for the Stairs of Cirith Ungol, and the watch-tower at the top as the model for the Tower of Cirith Ungol.

... but Gollum's eyes shone pale, several feet above, as he turned back towards them. 'Careful!' he whispered. 'Steps. Lots of steps. Must be careful!' Care was certainly needed. Frodo and Sam at first felt easier, having a wall on either side, but the stairway was almost as steep as a ladder, and as they climbed up and up, they became more and more aware of the long black fall behind them.

(*The Two Towers*, The Stairs of Cirith Ungol, J.R.R. Tolkien)

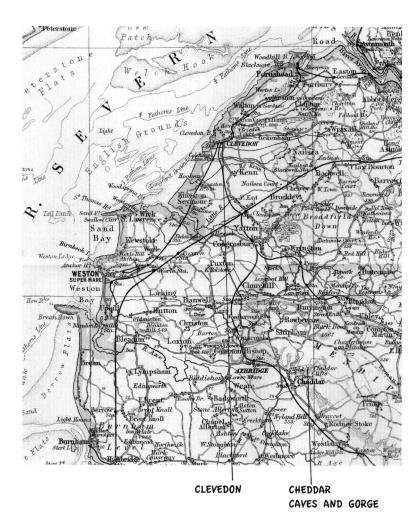

CLEVEDON

CHEDDAR CAVES AND GORGE

Map of North Somerset, showing Clevedon in the north and the Mendip Hills and Cheddar in the south; they are linked by a railway line.

A Meditation (On my beholding the Cheddar Cliffs)

My God who raised the Mendip Range
Out of the ocean bed,
And split and rent these hills that tower
So high above my head;
Who formed the Cheddar cliffs, and gave
Them beauties wondrous fair,
Whose power supports these pinnacles
That rise so high in air.
How I admire their beauteous forms,
Their Maker I adore;
Whenever I behold Thy works
I love Thee more and more.
Oh, may my love grow stronger
As I gaze upon the scene,
And if my life be longer spared
May clouds not come between.
That when my soul is called away
I leave this world with joy,
And live within the perfect light
Of bliss without alloy.
In seeming darkness Thou hast worked,
In caves unseen by man,
What wonders hast Thou brought to light,
In wisdom laid the plan;
But light and darkness are as one
To Thy all-searching eye
Though in creation but a mite
Thou doth not pass me by.
Make me, my God, in all things, as
Then would'st as I should be.
That while I live I evermore,
May praise and worship Thee.

(Richard Cox Gough, Cheddar Caves,
Cheddar, September 1898)

The towering cliffs at Cheddar Gorge. The road can be seen running through the bottom of the gorge.

The towering Pinnacles in Cheddar Gorge.

Still some miles away, on the far side of the Westfold Vale, lay a green coomb, a great bay in the mountains out of which a gorge opened in the hills. Men of that land called it Helm's Deep, after a hero of old wars who had made his refuge there.

(*The Two Towers*, Helm's Deep, J.R.R. Tolkien)

The River Avon running beside Warwick Castle. Ronald and Edith used to hire a punt on the river in the summer of 1913; they thought Warwick to be a place of beauty. The castle is believed to be the model for Dol Amroth Castle in *The Lord of the Rings*.

The Examination Schools, and University College (to the right of the schools, on the High Street), became the Third Southern Military Hospital during the war, as did many other colleges.

De Pary's Avenue, Bedford – a quiet, leafy suburb where Tolkien started his military training in July 1915.

The River Great Ouse flows through Bedford. Soldiers who were training there would have taken a turn along the embankment or a trip on a pleasure boat when off duty. The Anglo-Saxon King Offa of Mercia was buried here in AD 796.

Suspension Bridge, Bedford.

The suspension bridge across the River Great Ouse was built in 1888. It is an iron bowstring lattice girder bridge.

Royal Engineers using a field telephone somewhere on the Western Front.

After the war, Brocton Camp was closed and many of the army huts were sold. The hut in the picture is a survivor, having been a parish hall in the village of Gayton for around eighty-five years, some 10 miles away from Cannock Chase.

Opposite top: A fine modern summer view across Cannock Chase, in the area where Brocton Camp stood during the First World War. This would be a very bleak scene in the winter, with far fewer trees than today.

Opposite bottom: Brocton and Rugeley Camps were served by their own railway, with the train known as the Tackeroo Express – so-called because the branch line came off the London & North-Western main line near Tackeroo. The cutting shown shows the remains of the line, close to where the huge camp water tower / tank stood. It is returning to nature in a very Ent-like way.

The stove was the only form of heating in the huts, with the enlisted men having only one stove in the centre; but the officers' huts had several stoves each. The New Zealand flag shown in the picture is there because New Zealand troops were in the camp in 1917.

Opposite top: The hut was dismantled in May 2006, rebuilt in the spring of 2007, and now stands next to the Cannock Chase Visitors' Centre. It is partly fitted out to look as it would have done in 1916. This work was undertaken by a partnership of Friends of Cannock Chase and Staffordshire County Council.

Opposite bottom: The mess area of the hut, with enamel plates, jugs, mugs and bowls, all on wooden trestle tables with wooden benches to sit on. This would have been a soldier's home for the duration of his training at the camp, and most likely his last address in England before going overseas.

Brocton village stands a short distance from the huge military camp and gave its name to the camp.

On the edge of Brocton's village green stands half an army hut, most likely from Brocton Camp, which has been converted into a house.

The Cheddar Water or Cheddar Yeo, leaving Gough's Cave in the Cheddar Gorge.

A wall, too, the men of old had made from the Hornburg to the southern cliff, barring the entrance to the gorge. Beneath it by a wide culvert the Deeping Stream passed out.

(*The Two Towers*, Helm's Deep, J.R.R. Tolkien)

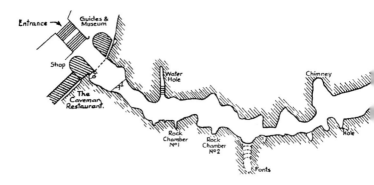

Map of Gough's Caves at
Cheddar Gorge.

Above: The view in Gough's Cave.

Still lakes mirror them; glimmering world up from dark pools covered with clear
glass, cities such as the mind of Durin could scarce have imagined in his sleep
stretch on through avenues and pillared courts, on into the dark recesses where
no light can come.

(*The Two Towers*, Helm's Deep, J.R.R. Tolkien)

Right: St Paul's at the Cheddar Caves, electrically illuminated.

And plink! A silver drop falls, and like weeds and corals in a grotto of the sea.

(*The Two Towers*, Helm's Deep, J.R.R. Tolkien)

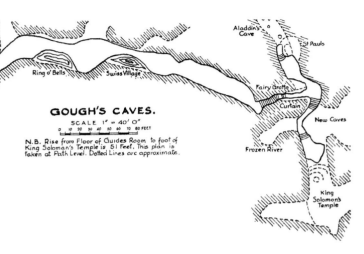

GOUGH'S CAVES.

SCALE 1" = 40' 0"

0 10 20 30 40 50 60 70 80 FEET

N.B. Rise from Floor of Guides Room to foot of King Soloman's Temple is 51 Feet. This plan is taken at Path Level. Dotted Lines are approximate.

Hole · Ring o' Bells · Swiss Village · Aladdin's Cave · St Pauls · Fairy Grotto · Curtain · New Caves · Frozen River · King Solomon's Temple

The view in Solomon's Temple, Cheddar Caves.

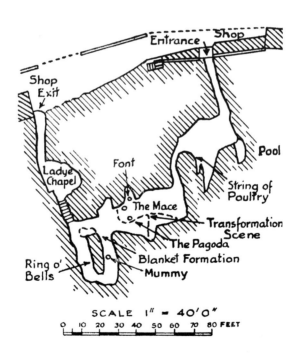

Map of Cox's Cave, Cheddar Gorge.

Cox's Cave.

And Legolas, when the torches are kindled and men walk on the sandy floors under the echoing domes, ah! then, Legolas, gems and crystals and veins of precious ore glinting in the polished walls; and the light glows through folded marbles, shell-like, translucent as the living hands of Queen Galadriel.

(*The Two Towers*, Helm's Deep, J.R.R. Tolkien)

Ronald and Edith returned to Warwick after their honeymoon and, after a short time, Ronald was posted to the Northern Command and Ripon Training Centre Signalling School at Farnley Park, Otley in Yorkshire, where he received training in signalling. By all reports he was pretty good at the academic side of signalling, in areas such as map reading and written tests, but a bit slow on the practical side, in areas such as using a signalling lamp. He was awarded a provisional certificate on 13 May that allowed him to train other soldiers in signalling.

8

Great Haywood

dith left Warwick and moved to the small village of Great Haywood, on the edge of Cannock Chase and close to Brocton Camp, so she could be close to Ronald while he was at the camp. Her cousin Jennie, who had been living with her in Warwick, also moved, so Edith would have some company for the long periods Ronald was on duty. They appear to have taken rooms in the presbytery attached to St John the Baptist Roman Catholic Church in Great Haywood. The church was in the Archdiocese of Birmingham, and maybe Father Francis had used the 'old-boys' priest network to get some safe, secure accommodation for the two young women. Accommodation was at a premium in the area, with so many soldiers' relatives wanting to spend time with their sons and husbands before they went off to fight, and the area was awash with soldiers taking a bit of leave.

As Edith and Ronald had married during Lent they could not have the Nuptial Mass after the wedding service, so this was undertaken at St John the Baptist Church in Great Haywood at Sunday mass.

Tolkien would have walked from Brocton Camp to Great Haywood and, on his route, he would have passed through the wild and sometimes bleak landscape of Cannon Chase, passing Brocton Coppice with its hundreds-of-years-old oak trees. (At the time of writing this book there has been an outbreak of Sudden Oak Death on the Chase; the disease also affects other plants and trees, so it may be worth checking if there are any restrictions on visiting Cannock Chase if you are planning a trip there.)

As Ronald approached Great Haywood, he would have passed by Shugborough Hall, with its grand front, columned terrace, matching wings and eighty chimneys! In 'The Tales of the Sun and the Moon' (*The Book of Lost Tales 1*), a gnome called Gilfanon owned a very old house, 'the House of a Hundred Chimneys', that stands by the Bridge of Tavrobel. A little further on, Tolkien would have come to the River Trent and crossed the river via Essex Bridge; a short distance up-river from the bridge, the River Sow joins the River Trent. In *The Book of Lost Tales 1*, Tolkien describes the village of Tavrobel as standing by the confluence of two rivers, with the Bridge of Tavrobel crossing the river. This could very well be Great Haywood and Essex Bridge.

After crossing the bridge and the canal, Tolkien would have passed under the railway close to Great Haywood station and into Trent Lane in the heart

SHUGBOROUGH HALL

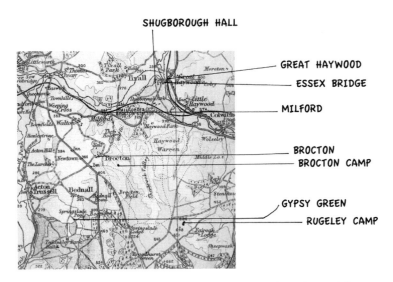

GREAT HAYWOOD

ESSEX BRIDGE

MILFORD

BROCTON
BROCTON CAMP

GYPSY GREEN
RUGELEY CAMP

Detailed map of the area around Cannock Chase, showing Great Haywood, Brocton, Milford and Teddesley Park in Staffordshire.

Shugborough Hall in Great Haywood was extensively enlarged in 1750. It was owned by the Earls of Lichfield and is now owned by Staffordshire County Council. It is open to the public.

of the village of Great Haywood. The old village is very little changed from the period that Edith and Ronald were there in lodgings, but the village as a whole has grown much in the twentieth century.

In early June, Ronald received orders that he was to join the British Expeditionary Force in France, and was granted a forty-eight-hour leave

Essex Bridge, in Great Haywood, links the village to Shugborough Hall and Park across the River Trent. The bridge was built in 1550 by the Earl of Essex for Queen Elizabeth I, to allow her to go hunting in the woodlands on the other side of the river when she visited the estate. With fourteen arches, it is the longest remaining packhorse bridge in England, and is a Grade I listed structure.

The Plough & Harrow Hotel on the Hagley Road, Edgbaston, Birmingham. Ronald and Edith stayed in room 116 on 3 June 1916. The view from the front of the hotel looks across to Highfield Road – the last place Tolkien and his brother Hilary had lodgings in Birmingham in 1911.

pass. He and Edith went to Birmingham and stayed at the Plough & Harrow Hotel on the Hagley Road on the Saturday night. This was the centre of their world during their teenage years when they started courting, with the Oratory just over the road and Duchess Road, where they first met, only a short walk away. On Sunday 4 June, Ronald was off to war. He said farewell

St John the Baptist Roman Catholic Church, Great Haywood, is part of the Archdiocese of Birmingham. It was originally built around 3 miles away, as a chapel for the Aston family at Tixall Hall in 1828; it was moved in 1845. The marks on the stone blocks, to allow correct reassembly, are still visible on the inside of the church.

to Edith before catching the train to London; this could have been their final parting as the death rate for officers on the Western Front was very high at the time. Edith no doubt returned to Great Haywood full of fear that this was the last time she would ever see Ronald again. The next day, Ronald took the train from Charing Cross station to Folkestone, where he reported to the Military Embarkation Staff and was most likely billeted in a local hotel overnight.

9

Prelude to the Somme

n 6 June, Ronald embarked for France from Folkestone Harbour on a troopship that could have been a converted liner or ferry; they would have been shepherded across the Channel by a destroyer escort. This must have been a lonely time for Ronald, as he was travelling alone whereas most soldiers were travelling in the units that they had trained with, and many soldiers were in 'pals' battalions that had been recruited from a single town or city.

The troopship docked safely at Le Havre and Ronald travelled to the massive army camps at Étaples, which the soldiers called eat-apples, and he was billeted in camp 32. The military camps around Étaples were massive, with accommodation for around 100,000 troops (much of which was in tents), sixteen hospitals and convalescent depots, reinforcement camps for commonwealth troops, and barracks for the French Army.

During Tolkien's voyage across the English Channel or on route to the camp, most of his sleeping gear and a spare pair of boots had gone astray or been stolen, so he had to scrounge or buy replacements for them. The next day, Tolkien was moved to camp 25; this camp was where rookie troops for the front were given their front line training and hardened up for the rigours of trench warfare. The whole area had a poor reputation with the

A ferry docking at Folkestone Harbour to meet the troop train.

HMS *Lurcher* was the type of destroyer that would have escorted the troopship or ferry on which Tolkien travelled across the English Channel. HMS *Lurcher* was launched in 1912 and at the time was the fastest ship in the Royal Navy. She was sold for scrap in 1922.

A ferry heading out into the Channel at Le Havre.

soldiers and the most notorious place was the Bull Ring, a training camp in the sand dunes at Étaples. This was most likely where Tolkien undertook his training. Here, up to 20,000 soldiers could be drilled or given lectures at the same time on lice, trench foot and poison gas.

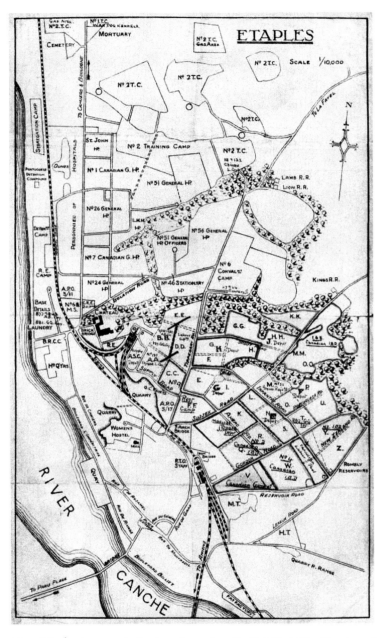

Map of the Étaples camps in Northern France from the First World War. (Courtesy of the First World War Poetry Digital Archive, University of Oxford)

Trench foot was caused by soldiers having to stand in water and suffering damp feet for long periods of time. Their feet could turn red or blue and, in the worst cases, this could lead to gangrene and the amputation of the foot or feet. The British and French trenches on the Western Front were often waterlogged. This was because, in 1914, once the stalemate of trench-warfare began, the Germans withdrew to the higher ground to dig their trench defensive systems. It was a bit like they were building a castle wall from the North Sea to Switzerland, but instead of building walls upwards, they were digging in trenches and dugouts. The Allies were left in many cases with their trench systems in the lower ground. Even if the German trenches did flood, the Germans would pump the water out and it would flow down to the Allied trenches. There was often human waste in the water. To overcome this problem, trenches were fitted with raised wooden walkways called 'duck-boards'.

The hospitals at Étaples had a poor reputation; it was even said that some men in the hospitals would prefer to return to their units at the front after a couple of weeks rather than stay in the hospitals. The Étaples camps were the location of the first British Army mutiny in September 1917. Wilfred Owen wrote to his mother about the camp in December 1917:

> Last year I lay awake in a windy tent in the middle of a vast, dreadful encampment. It seemed neither France nor England but a kind of paddock where beasts are kept a few days before the shambles ... I thought of the very strange look on all faces in the camp; an incomprehensible look, which a man will never see in England, though wars should be in England; nor can it be seen in any battle. But only in Etaples.
>
> (*Collected Letters*, Wilfred Owen,
> ed. H. Owen and J. Bell)

Tolkien's relationship with the enlisted men was one of mutual respect. However, many of them would have been poorly educated and working class, and most officers came from privileged backgrounds and were at least grammar school educated. Some of the officers were as young as eighteen or nineteen years old. It would have been frowned upon for Tolkien to strike up a friendship with the enlisted men, but he would have had a batman whom he would work closely with. This kind of relationship can be seen in the master/servant/friend relationship in *The Lord of the Rings* between Frodo and Sam, and Tolkien's officer experience is likely to be one of its roots.

Tolkien disliked his senior officers who were tough and hardened to the rigours of war, and he felt they treated him and other junior officers like schoolboys. As many of the junior officers were actually just out of school, the senior officers may have been trying to save their lives by toughening

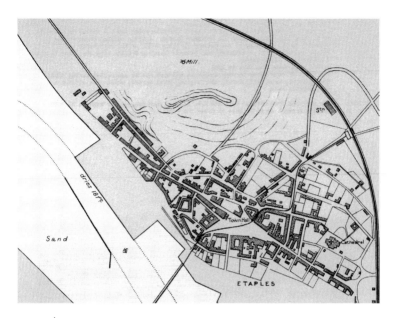

Map of Étaples town.

Fishing boats in the estuary at Étaples, France.

them up. Tolkien was also writing at the time but had no one to talk to about it, perhaps feeling that writing poetry would be looked down upon by enlisted men and officers alike. Despite any differences between the men, they were all in the same boat, and would sink or swim together by their actions at the front.

The entire time that Tolkien was in the camps, the place was awash with rumours of the 'big push' that was to take place close to the town

A street scene from the once quiet seaside town of Étaples, where the British Army set up a huge army camp in the sand dunes. The town name has been crudely crossed out on the postcard; this was a common form of censorship for postcards sent home from France by the troops.

of Albert in the Somme region of Northern France, and tales of spies were commonplace. Tolkien wrote to Edith back at Great Haywood most days but, because of the censorship imposed on the letters, he found little he could write about his daily life other than the weather, which at the time was very poor for the time of year. So that Edith could keep track of his movements in France, he had invented a code of dots; Edith could thus pinpoint his location in France from the dots and plot his location on the map of France she had on the wall in her lodgings in Great Haywood.

On 27 June, Tolkien finally got his orders to join the 11th Lancashire Fusiliers. By this time the weather was hot and the heat was causing thunderstorms, but some days earlier the distant 'thunder' heard was caused by the bombardment on the German positions at the Somme. It was said that at the start of the bombardment, the glass in windows in the south of England started to rattle.

Tolkien travelled by train to Abbeville, and then by train down the river valley of the Somme to the cathedral city of Amiens. The valley in summer is a very beautiful place, with marshy lowlands and banks lined with willow and alder trees. Amiens was awash with troops – phalanxes of British cavalry with their flat-caps, sabres and carbines, and Indian cavalry with their black beards and blue turbans. Marching through the city were troops from Bermuda, Newfoundland, New Zealand, Australia, South Africa, Canada and the British Army. Many were mere boys on their first trip abroad; countless numbers of them were never to return home again. Here Tolkien ate a meal from an army field kitchen in the town square, with the backdrop of the great Amiens Cathedral to study before setting off to join his unit at Rubempré, some 14km north-east of Amiens.

He was passing through the rich countryside of Picardy, with fields and orchards laden with their forthcoming harvests – but in many of the fields,

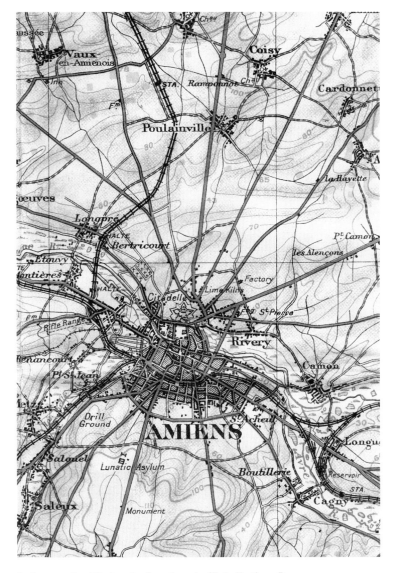

Amiens was the Allies' centre for railway traffic in Northern France.

Amiens Cathedral. The spire masonry is much more elaborate than the spire at Exeter College Chapel. The cathedral survived the Battle of Amiens in August 1918 with little damage, due to the protection of many thousands of sandbags.

men and horses parked up awaiting their call to the front. Tolkien arrived at the farming village of Rubempré in a heavy downpour of rain to join about 800 men of the 11th Lancashire Fusiliers who were billeted in the barns and outbuildings of the village. The rain was going to cause a delay in the attack on the Somme; the planned date for the start of the battle was supposed to be 28 June, but this was postponed until 1 July, a date that was going to become infamous in the history of the British Army. And, all the time, the big guns were thundering away in the background to soften up the German positions on the front line.

The next day, 29 June, the battalion knuckled down to serious training to get into shape for the forthcoming battle; they had an hour of physical training, bayonet practice, drill and then 'on the double' marching. The battalion could be said to be a bit of a scratch unit, as many in the army were at the time. A handful of officers – like Tolkien – were new to the unit, around twenty-five per cent of the enlisted men were newly trained recruits, and the rest of the men had been in France for almost a year. Many of the older officers, most likely called up from the reserve, had only fought in colonial wars in the British Empire. Tolkien gave signalling training to some of the men and, the following day, the battalion trained again. In the evening they moved camp and marched eastwards towards the gunfire. They were billeted in the village of Warloy-Baillon, some 11km behind the front line.

The Jules Verne monument in Amiens. It is nice to think that Tolkien marched past this monument to the father of science fiction, as he was to become the father of fantasy fiction in later life.

10

The Battle of the Somme

he Battle of the Somme has its roots in December 1915, when the east and west Allies held a conference at Chantilly in France to coordinate their offensives. The Allies had attempted to attack Germany via the 'backdoor' in 1915 at Gallipoli in Turkey, but this had failed and losses on the Western Front were very high as well. This led to conscription for single men in January 1916. Sir Douglas Haig, Commander-in-Chief of the British Expeditionary Forces, had chosen Flanders for the planned assault on the German lines. This may appear to be a strange choice, as this sector of the line had been relatively quiet for the last two years and the Germans had not been idle in constructing strong defensive positions there. John Masefield, who had been a hospital orderly in France in the early phases of the war and was to become the Poet Laureate in 1930, wrote about a visit to the front line:

> Almost in every part our men had to go uphill to attack ... The enemy had look-out posts with fine views ... Our men were down below with no view of anything but stronghold after stronghold just up above being made stronger daily.

Another reason for the Battle of the Somme was to relieve the pressure on the French Army at Verdun; this battle started on 21 February 1916 and finished on 18 December 1916. The losses in this battle were staggering: 163,000 French killed, 141,000 Germans killed and around half a million wounded.

Preparations for the Battle of the Somme – or, as it was known at the time, the Battle of Albert – were vast in terms of both men and materials. Railway lines and light railways were built to aid the flow of supplies to the front, tons of shells (some of poison gas) were stockpiled, and tons of fodder was stockpiled to feed the cavalry horses and the army of horses required to tow the artillery and supply wagons. Whole villages were evacuated of their civilian populations, hundreds of miles of telephone cable was laid underground, and, as June rolled on, more and more troops poured into the area. The whole place must have looked like a giant anthill.

One task that was going on deep underground was the digging of mines under the German lines – when the British Army had taken over the Somme

The night scene on the Somme, 1 July 1916. The arcs of tracer shells can be seen rising from the guns and falling on the German positions. These would have been used to show the artillery spotters where the shells were falling.

STAR SHELL BURSTING NEAR BRITISH LINES.

A shell-burst close to the British line at night.

OH! THE TROUBLE THESE THINGS
HAVE CAUSED !

A Fred Spurgin postcard condemning the trouble caused by the big guns. Up to eighty per cent of the casualties on the Western Front were caused by shelling, with soldiers literally being blown to smithereens.

sector of the front from the French, they had inherited a number of active mines. The chalk rock of this region was ideal for tunnelling through, but this was a war within a war; there was equipment for listening for the other side's tunnelling sounds, soldiers blowing up the other side's tunnels, and even hand-to-hand fighting in the tunnel systems. Many of the men involved in this work had been miners in the coal and tin industries before the war, and were nicknamed 'the moles' by the other troops. Companies of men had worked together digging sewers and railway tunnels under British cities; they had finished work on a Friday, been called to arms, and were working in France by the Monday morning. The men digging the tunnels were also called 'clay kickers' and were working in a three-shift system, covering twenty-four hours each day. Some of the men working on the tunnels were comparatively well paid, getting six shillings a day compared to an infantryman whose pay was one shilling a day. At the end of each tunnel there was a chamber packed with ammonal explosive, with command wires from the detonators leading back to a safe firing location. This method of undermining the enemy's defences goes back to at least the medieval age, and most likely a lot further back than that.

The delaying of the start date due to rain put the British Army at the Somme under great pressure. Units moving up to the front with their home-made flags and banners were taken off the road. They were told to bivouac in fields, coppices and abandoned villages, and find what shelter

Troops marching to the front. In the First World War, the infantry soldiers marched huge distances because of the lack of motorised transport at the time. This is a stage-managed picture for the press.

they could. In some of the villages, slogans were daubed on the walls by the troops who had already moved up to the front line; these stated such things as 'Now for Berlin' and 'Look Out Kaiser Bill'. The troops on the front line were having much greater problems – their trenches were filling up with water and, because the British artillery barrage had slackened, especially the heavy guns, the German batteries had started shelling the British front line trenches. The troops in these trenches were taking heavy casualties and were going to have to endure this for the next forty-eight hours.

Raiding parties were sent out to assess the damage to the German front line defences and came back with disturbing reports. They found that in some places the barbed-wire was still in place and uncut, and the defences were not being destroyed by the shelling. Around 1.5 million shells had been fired at the German positions, but one third were duds and the barbed-wire-cutting shrapnel shells, which were filled with ball bearings that exploded out of the shell, had also failed to cut the wire. However, the Germans were lying low in deep dugouts, so the raiding parties thought that the bombardment had destroyed them.

German barbed-wire and wooden spikes protecting a German trench. The German barbed-wire was a much heavier gauge than the British wire. Barbed-wire was first patented in the United States in 1867 by Lucien B. Smith of Ohio, and was used as cheap fencing material to control cattle. It was extensively used in the Boer War by the British Army.

During the night of 30 June, more and more troops moved up to the front line, and reserve trenches were packed with troops to follow on after the first waves of men had gone over the top into no-man's-land. Behind the lines, the massed ranks of cavalry were preparing to charge forward through the hoped-for breaches that the infantry were going to create in the German lines. The cavalry would have looked more at home in a war from the nineteenth century.

The 1st of July dawned. The rain had gone and the sun was shining; it looked like being a fine summer's day once the low mist had burned away. Tolkien was still billeted in the village of Warloy-Baillon behind the front line. Just after dawn, the British artillery started its final bombardment and, at about 6.30 a.m., the artillery started to increase its rate of firing; the world around the front line was deafened by a thunderous roar. At 7.20, the first mine was detonated under Hawthorn Ridge, and a further eight mines were detonated at 7.28 at strong points under the German front line. The three largest mines had over 20 tons of ammonal explosive packed into each chamber, and the smaller mines had around 5,000lb of explosive each – this was, at the time, the largest man-made explosion on the planet. The mine at Kasino Point was mistimed, and exploded during the infantry advance.

The explosions from the mines rocked the British front line; the concussion killed many German troops in their trenches and dugouts, and blasted hundreds of tons of earth and chalk thousands of feet into the air. Chalk dust fell to the ground like snow and the explosions were heard as far away as London.

> And even as he spoke the earth rocked beneath their feet. Then rising swiftly up, far above the Tower of the Black Gate, high above the mountains, a vast soaring darkness sprang into the sky, flickering with fire. The earth groaned and quaked.
>
> (*The Return of the King*, The Field of Cormallen,
> J.R.R. Tolkien)

A 7.30 a.m. the whistles were blown and, with hope and courage, the first wave of men climbed out of the relative safety of their trenches into no-man's-land; many were with their pals, brothers and workmates, buoyed up by their early morning tot of rum.

Many of the more experienced officers had moved their troops into no-man's-land as the German counter-barrage was about to start up on the front line trenches. Many officers were not wearing their officer uniform but were dressed as privates to reduce the chance of being shot by a German sniper; this was the case with Tolkien's friend Ron Gilson, who

A British mine exploding under the German lines at the start of the Battle of the Somme.

The British mine exploding at Beaumont-Hamel on 1 July 1916 at 7.28 a.m. The mine contained 18 tons of ammonal explosive.

was in the third wave going over the top some two and a half minutes after the first wave. A few minutes later, Gilson was killed by a shell-burst, and is buried in Becourt Cemetery.

The troops advancing towards the German trenches were doing so at a steady walking pace, spaced about six arm's-lengths apart in waves of two platoons at a time; this had all been set out in a pamphlet called the 'Fourth Army Tactical Notes' for the troops. The advancing troops were burdened with at least 70lb/32kg of equipment, including a tin-hat (a pressed steel helmet), rifle with the bayonet fixed, ammunition, two grenades, wire cutters,

*Sketches
of Tommy's life*
Up the line -- N° 7

One of the bright spots in our life.

Visé Paris 763

Dawn was considered the most likely time for an enemy attack, so all the troops in the front line trenches would stand-to. After stand-to, the troops would be given their daily rum ration, which was two tablespoons. The earthenware rum jars had the letters SRD on them, which stood for Supply Reserve Depot – but the soldiers joked that SRD stood for Seldom Reaches Destination.

entrenching tool, empty sandbags, flares, first-aid kit and a water-bottle. Some of the later waves carried even more equipment, for consolidating captured German trenches, such as barbed-wire and iron stakes. Carrying that amount of weight into battle meant that running or crawling was not really practical, and so walking was judged to be the best option.

As the troops advanced across no-man's-land flying their home-made banners, kicking footballs and cheering loudly, 'all hell was let loose' from the German trenches, which were quite damaged but still serviceable. Machine guns on the sometimes shattered parapets were rattling and spitting as they scythed through the waves of men advancing towards them. Shells from the little-damaged German artillery were bursting overhead and trench mortars were spraying out a deadly hail of shrapnel, cutting down the troops as they tried to advance.

The Germans had seemed to come back from the dead, as the British troops had thought that the bombardment had blasted them 'to kingdom come'. When the bombardment lifted from the German lines, the troops came up from their deep bunkers and manned the trenches, although some of them must have lost their minds during the shelling. They were faced with lines of infantry moving slowly towards them in an unbroken line, as if they were on manoeuvres. As well as fighting for Germany and the Kaiser,

The black dots at the top of the picture are troops advancing through the blasted wasteland of no-man's-land on 1 July 1916, at the start of the Battle of the Somme.

the German soldiers were fighting for their comrades in the line and for their own lives.

The 'big push' had failed in most cases to break through the German line; men had been driven back to their own trenches if they were lucky, and thousands lay dead and dying in no-man's-land or were hung up like macabre scarecrows on the German spider's web-like barbed-wire entanglements.

> 'Cobwebs!' he said. 'Is that all? Cobwebs! But what a spider! Have at 'em, down with 'em!' In a fury he hewed at them with his sword, but the thread that struck did not break. It gave a little and then sprang back like a plucked bowstring, turning the blade and tossing up both sword and arm. Three times Sam struck with all his force and at last one single cord of all the countless cords snapped and twisted.
>
> (*The Two Towers*, Shelob's Lair, J.R.R. Tolkien)

It is said that there were literally piles of dead and dying British soldiers in the front of the German lines.

> Not though the walls be taken by a reckless foe that will build a hill of carrion before them.
>
> (*The Return of the King*, Minas Tirith, J.R.R. Tolkien)

German soldiers playing cards behind the lines. It could almost be a group of Hobbits resting while on a ramble in the woods.

A German soldier on cooking duty behind the lines. The form of a woman is rising from his pan – perhaps wistful thinking?

Many men were killed later in the day when the Germans systematically machine-gunned no-man's-land, killing the exposed wounded and isolated pockets of trapped soldiers. The first day of the Battle of the Somme had been the greatest disaster in the history of the British Army, with 19,240 dead, 35,493 wounded, 2,152 missing and 585 taken prisoner. This was to be

German guns captured at the Battle of the Somme.

a greater tragedy on a different level, as many of the battalions were Pals battalions, and these men had enlisted from a single town or city. The Battle of the Somme therefore led to the loss of practically a whole generation from some towns, cities or streets, and in some cases it took many days to print all their pictures and obituaries in the local newspapers.

The French to the south had not started fighting till 9.30 a.m. and, because of Verdun, the Germans were not expecting an attack. The French advanced in small groups, using the river mist and folds in the landscape as cover, and each group could give covering fire to help their neighbouring groups. They overran the German positions with relatively light casualties.

On Sunday 2 July, Tolkien attended an open-air mass; the chaplain was from the Royal Irish Rifles. Rumours were that the attack had smashed the German front line but the signs were not good; endless streams of traffic taking the wounded back could be seen on the roads. The official word about the battle was that progress had been slow. The fighting was still going on and the casualties on the second day were around 30,000.

Tolkien and the Lancashire Fusiliers were held in reserve, but on Monday 3 July they were ordered to move to the village of Bouzincourt about 8km away. As they left in the early evening, a battered Highland Division covered in the chalk mud from the Somme battlefield struggled past them.

In the morning, the area around Bouzincourt came under fire from the German artillery. The men were billeted in the village buildings and under the trees in the nearby orchards; the village was not damaged in the shelling. Heavy, thunderous rain started pouring down and the men who were not undercover in the village got soaked as they had to stay put for fear of being spotted by a German plane.

ROLL CALL, COUNTING THE DEAD, SOMME 1916

Roll call for the Lancashire Fusiliers after the first day of the Battle of the Somme. Each soldier is deep in thought as the names of the dead, wounded and missing are called out, to be answered with a dead silence. (Courtesy of Soren Hawkes MA)

HIGHLANDERS PIPE THEMSELVES BACK FROM THE TRENCHES

Highland soldiers piping themselves back from the front line trenches along a sunken road.

Tolkien and 11th Lancashire Fusiliers were in the reserve at Bouzincourt behind the front lines, having moved there on 3 July 1916. This picture was taken of the village after it had been bombarded by German artillery.

A graveyard where soldiers are being buried. A chaplain, the figure in white, is conducting the burial services.

Many wounded men were brought back to the village to have their wounds dressed before being sent to the hospitals well behind the front lines, and then sent back to Britain by hospital ship. The industrial nature of this modern warfare caused hideous damage to the bodies of the wounded soldiers who had survived the fighting of the last few days.

Tolkien and the men of his battalion were still training, and supplying troops for work parties to dig graves for the ever-growing cemetery – not the best morale booster for men who were shortly to go into battle.

An army chaplain tending the fresh graves of British soldiers on the Western Front.

On the Wednesday, orders came for the whole of Tolkien's brigade to go and reinforce the brigade fighting at La Boisselle; they left on Thursday, 6 July. Tolkien remained behind with other signal officers, to help operate the communications for the entire 25th Division. The same day, his friend from the TCBS, Geoffrey Smith, turned up fresh from the fighting in which nearly fifty per cent of the platoon had not returned. Over the next few days, Tolkien and Smith spent some time together. They talked about poetry, the war and things to come.

The Bouzincourt signals office had been damaged by shellfire on 6 July and there was a steady flow of wounded soldiers coming into the village. On the Saturday, Smith departed with the Salford Pals to join in with the continuing attack on Ovillers.

On Monday 10 July, the battered remains of the 11th Lancashire Fusiliers returned to Bouzincourt and, after a very short space of time, they moved out to the village of Senlis, which was a further 2km behind the front line. Here they were to rest up and get prepared for their next set of orders, which came on 14 July.

11

Into Battle

On the morning of 15 July, the Lancashire Fusiliers marched out of the village, back through Bouzincourt and along the Ancre Valley. The road was packed with a mixture of military traffic, old and new together – modern motorised vehicles alongside the more traditional horse-drawn wagons, pack mules and marching troops. In the field beside the road more troops were resting up and, as Tolkien got closer to the town of Albert, the flashes from the heavy artillery hammering away at the German lines came into view.

Standing tall and defiant was the devastated remains of the Basilica in the centre of Albert, towering over the shell-shattered town. On top of the Basilica tower, the Golden Virgin and Child glinted in the sunlight. They had been blown off their perch by shelling in January 1915 and had been secured with cable by French troops. Troops on both sides thought that the war would end when the statue fell down – and it finally came down, a circumstance caused by British shellfire, three months before the Armistice in 1918.

Tolkien's brigade marched around the northern suburbs of Albert and bivouacked by a stream running off the chalk downs that rose steadily towards the front line. Running through the landscape was the old Roman road, ploughing a very straight line, and the area was awash with troops

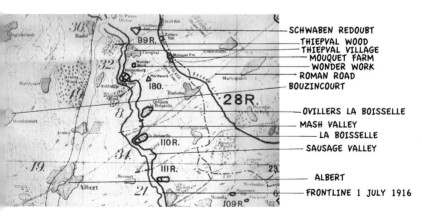

Map of the area of the Battle of the Somme where Tolkien and 11th Lancashire Fusiliers fought and were billeted in 1916.

King George V inspecting a heavy artillery gun on the Western Front during the First World War.

Albert before the start of the First World War. The Basilica towers high above the town, a dominant landmark in the surrounding landscape.

bivouacking in the surrounding fields. Some were even asleep in fox-holes or shell-holes, as the area was sometimes coming under German artillery fire. In the afternoon, Tolkien learnt that he was going into battle or, as they would have said at the time, 'the show'. This always makes it sound as though they were off to the music hall, but more likely they were off to the theatre of death. There was another theatre connection, however, as by this time in the war a number of music hall stars were working as nurses in hospitals in France. Tolkien's platoon was teamed up with the Royal Irish, a regular army unit, and, as they marched towards the front, the great tear

Left: The Basilica in Albert, topped by the Golden Virgin and Child (before the First World War).

Below left: The Basilica was heavily shelled in the January of 1915; the Golden Virgin and Child collapsed.

Top right: The inside of the Basilica after the bombardment.

Bottom right: The Great Altar in the Basilica after the bombardment.

British troops bivouacking in fox-holes dug into chalky subsoil. They are filling sandbags and placing them at the head end of the fox-hole to give a little extra protection.

Looking into the massive crater caused by a mine exploding under La Boisselle, 1 July 1916. The tunnel entrance on the left of the picture is most likely the remains of the tunnel dug by the miners under the German front line. The pathways through the crater show that this picture was taken well after the explosion.

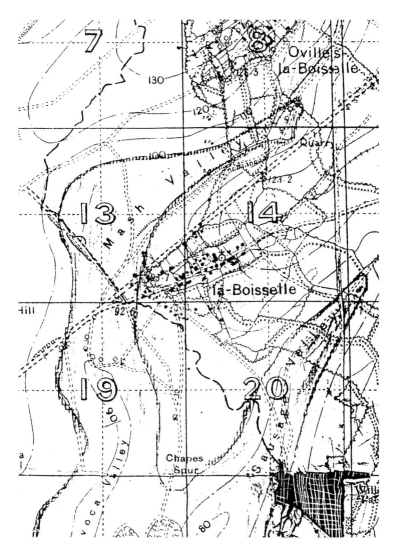

Map of Ovillers and La Boisselle, showing the lay of the land. Sausage Valley, shown on the map, had a twin valley a short distance away called Mash Valley. (OS sheet 57D)

in the landscape caused by a mine on 1 July came into view on the right. On the left was Ovillers, higher than the surrounding countryside, a salient jutting out from the chalk downs and still held by the Germans.

Tolkien now marched through the shell-shattered village of La Boisselle, which had been captured on 4 July 1916. The fighting had been intense and sometimes hand-to-hand, and many thousands of men on both sides of the line were dead or wounded; the British had fought from trenches sometimes knee-deep or even waist-deep in slimy mud.

Tolkien and the Lancashire Fusiliers now entered a deep, captured German trench system that had stood up to the bombardment remarkably well. Much of it had been constructed by the forced labour of Russian prisoners of war from the Eastern Front. As Tolkien got closer to the front line, the smell of death was in the air and dead bodies littered the landscape; bodies bloated in the summer heat were now being fed on by nature's recycling agents – maggots and trench rats.

British troops going over the top amid bursting gas and shells, in a determined assault on fortified Somme villages.

CLEVEDON

THE GEM OF SUNNY SOMERSET

ILLUSTRATED GUIDE POST FREE FROM
"PUBLICITY" COUNCIL HOUSE, CLEVEDON
CHEAP MONTHLY RETURN TICKETS ISSUED DAILY

A Great Western Railway poster for the Somerset resort of Clevedon.
(Courtesy of Dalkeith Publishing Co.)

A fine view across Essex Bridge at Great Haywood, with the track at the end of the bridge leading to Great Haywood village.

Great Haywood High Street is little changed since the First World War, when Edith Tolkien was lodging there to be close to Ronald.

The stylish church tower at St John the Baptist Roman Catholic Church, Great Haywood.

Amiens Cathedral, viewed from the river. Perhaps the spire reminded Tolkien of the spire of Exeter College in Oxford.

AMMUNITION CONVOY ON THE SOMME

A heavily laden ammunition convoy plodding to the artillery positions behind the front lines, to stock and feed the ever-hungry guns. There would have been hundreds of such convoys in the lead-up to the Battle of the Somme, and horse power was still the main method of transport at the time.

A British heavy artillery gun in action. On the left of the picture, a soldier is removing the shells from their canisters; next to him a soldier is priming the shells, all overseen by an officer.

BRITISH HEAVY GUN IN ACTION

The Golden Virgin and Child, photographed from the air by an early aeroplane or airship from before the First World War.

A mural in Albert showing a scene from 1916. Troops are passing the shell-damaged Basilica, with the Golden Virgin and Child leaning at a very precarious angle. The restored Basilica tower, with Golden Virgin and Child, shines above the mural. (Courtesy of Dave Sumpner)

Excavated trenches at Thiepval Wood on the Somme. (Courtesy of No Man's Land, The European Group for Great War Archaeology)

Excavated trenches at Thiepval Wood on the Somme. (Courtesy of No Man's Land, The European Group for Great War Archaeology)

Ted Nasmith's wonderful picture, 'Gollum's Debate'. To my eyes, Ted has created a vision of a shell-hole in the blasted wastes of Mordor. Tolkien has said that Mordor was based on his experiences in the shell-blasted wasteland of the trenches in 1916. (Courtesy of Ted Nasmith. For more information, visit www.tednasmith. com)

Lighthouse, Withernsea

Withernsea, on the North Sea coast in Yorkshire. The lighthouse was most likely not in use during the war, as it would have been a beacon for the German Navy.

Gypsy Green, viewed from the end of the private track which leads to it. Ronald and Edith rented a house in Gypsy Green during the First World War as it was close to the camps on Cannock Chase. It remains today a very isolated little hamlet in the Staffordshire countryside.

French engineers laying telephone cables through a shattered village. It would not be hard to tap these phone lines at night.

A shell-shattered village on the Somme after days of bombardment by the British artillery.

The entrance to a captured German dugout at La Boisselle, still intact. Beyond is the smashed-up German barbed-wire – still looking like a formable barrier – and the shell-potted landscape. The low ground at the top of the picture is where the British troops attacked from. The tiny figure in the top left of the picture gives you an idea of the scale of the destruction.

British troops relaxing in a trench. The holes cut into the side of the trench were sleeping holes, known as 'pozzies'.

A captured German deep dugout. This was not some hand-dug trench, but a deep, concreted fortification that was constructed to survive a heavy bombardment. The picture was taken at Ovillers.

Tolkien and the Fusiliers were now in the reserve trenches and fighting was raging above them in Ovillers, but this attack around midnight was beaten back and, around 2 a.m., Tolkien's unit was called upon to join the survivors of the first assault for a further attack. Thousands of men over the past two weeks had been sacrificed on the altar of the German defences of Ovillers. They were to attack through a hideous, man-made bramble patch of barbed-wire covering the shattered, terraced landscape – which was riddled with shell-holes from the British bombardment and swept by German machine-gun fire.

Tolkien was in charge of communications – a thankless task at the time – in captured front line positions on the Somme; surface cables had been run from La Boisselle to the forward positions at Ovillers. His job was to get information back to the commanders behind the lines so they could form a picture of how the fighting was going, and take action with re-enforcements or bring down artillery fire to support the attacking troops. As it was then, and is now, information on the battlefield is power.

The attack was called off and Tolkien returned to La Boisselle, where he spent the following night in a deep, captured German bunker that even had electrical lighting. These were a far cry from the British bunkers that were literally holes in the side of a trench.

There was a further attack on Ovillers the following night but Tolkien's battalion was in reserve; the Germans were still putting up stiff resistance and the attack once again failed. However, a battalion from the Warwickshires had captured the supply trench that linked the Germans in Ovillers with their rear lines, and the defenders in Ovillers were now cut off. The Warwickshires were pinned down all day by sniper fire and

German soldiers advancing through a shell-shattered landscape after a bombardment.

A captured German trench at Ovillers. The soldiers are from the Cheshire Regiment; a number are sleeping, exhausted by the battle they have just fought. A nice bit of wattle revetment on the left-hand side of the trench seems strangely out of place in a mechanical war, but would have held the wall of the trench up very well.

Shattered German trenches after the bombardment and capture of Ovillers in July 1916. The almost flat landscape that the British had crossed can be seen at the top of the picture.

hand-thrown bombs; Tolkien's brigade was given the task of reinforcing the Warwickshires but did not undertake any suicidal charges across open ground, instead giving logistical support to the Royal Irish. As the evening drew on, Tolkien's battalion led a successful attack on Ovillers, and the battered and cut-off Germans raised a white flag and surrendered; all of the 126 officers and men who surrendered were unwounded. Had it been daylight, the view back towards the original British line from the higher ground of Ovillers would have resembled a scene from hell, with the shell-potted landscape littered with the dead from the last sixteen days of fierce fighting. Tolkien and the Fusiliers returned to Bouzincourt in the early hours of 17 July; they had been fighting for just over two days.

12

The Daily Grind of War

or Tolkien and the survivors of the 11th Lancashire Fusiliers, life was now to turn into a strange routine of going up-the-line to fight for a few days or hours and then going back into reserve; training and drilling and then going back to the front line again. This was also the case for most British troops in the Somme area. But the high command was not about to give up the fight at this point, even though they had not made the breach that had been planned, for they were still going to shell the German lines in the hope that they would eventually break through. However, lessons had been learnt – at great cost to the lives of the soldiers – and methods of attack and bombardment had consequently been changed; some changes had also been made in the middle levels of the army's leadership.

At Bouzincourt, the Fusiliers and Tolkien slept and had a well-deserved rest before marching off to Forceville, where they bivouacked overnight before setting off the next day to Beauval, where they rested up. Here they undertook training, reorganisation (following the losses of the last few days of fighting) and were inspected.

On 21 July, Tolkien was appointed battalion signal officer; he was now in charge of a large group of men who ranged from runners to telephone operators and, in this mobile war, they had to set up communications as and when the battalion moved around the battlefield.

On Sunday 23 July, Tolkien attended a Roman Catholic service. On Monday 24, Tolkien and the Fusiliers moved back up into the front line trenches at Beaumont-Hamel and Auchonvillers; they stayed there till 29 July. During this time, they worked on improving and enlarging the trench system, reinforcing the barbed-wire defences, and repairing the communications infrastructure. A new steel-armoured communication cable was laid to the old front line, to carry the telephone and Morse code messages back to headquarters. The trenches were occasionally shelled by the Germans, causing the deaths of six men.

On Sunday 30 July at 4 a.m., Tolkien and the Fusiliers were relieved and moved out of the front line to become part of the division's reserve, bivouacking in a wood at Mailly-Maillet. Here they took part in a parade, on 1 August, to celebrate a victory over the French in 1759, took baths, and had a bit of 'rest and relaxation' (R and R) in the form of an inter-company 'sports day' – tug-of-war, relay-racing and a concert. From 2 until 4 August they were still in the reserve, carrying out more drilling and training, and work parties were digging trenches and dugouts. On 5 August, Tolkien and the Fusiliers left their reserve duties and marched off to a camp at Bertrancourt, where they spent the next two nights in tents. On Sunday 6 August, Tolkien attended a Roman Catholic service there.

On 7 August, Tolkien and the Fusiliers moved back into the front line trenches opposite Beaumont-Hamel, by the village of Colincamps. Over the next couple of days they were working on repairing the trench system – sometimes under fire from the Germans – and suffered eight casualties, four of whom were killed. On 10 August they were relieved by the 1st Welsh Guards and marched to Bus-les-Artois, where they spent the next five days once again drilling, training, bathing, having inspections and holding boxing competitions.

On 15 August, Tolkien and the Fusiliers were on the move again; they marched to Acheux-en-Amiénois where they once again undertook training, moving to the front line trenches at Thiepval on 20 August. But Tolkien was not with them, as he had been sent on a course for battalion

The French 75s moving up during the attack on Thiepval Ridge, passing German prisoners taken from the attack on the Wonder Work.

signalling officers from 16 to 23 August. The First World War was a war of technology and training, and new or improved techniques in all areas of warfare – such as signalling – could give soldiers the edge over their enemy in the fighting in the trenches. During the course, Tolkien met up and dined with his old school friend Geoffrey Smith at Bouzincourt; the village came under German shellfire while they were eating.

By 24 August, Tolkien had rejoined the 11th Lancashire Fusiliers in the trenches in the wood near to Thiepval. The British attack on the Somme had, by this time, become focused on the village of Thiepval and the defensive position known as the Schwaben Redoubt. The Fusiliers were not directly involved in the fighting at this time but were constructing new trenches, sometimes under German shellfire; they were relieved on 26 August and marched back to Bouzincourt.

Tolkien and the Fusiliers returned to the front line in trenches north of Ovillers, by the Leipzig Salient, in the early hours of the morning of 28 August. Once again they were working to repair and reinforce the trench system but were hampered by the trenches being flooded (due to downpours of rain) and shelling. Five men were killed and thirty were wounded. Tolkien was overseeing the installation of new signal cables that ran back to the Brigade Headquarters. On 1 September they were relieved from the front line trenches and moved back into the reserve trenches, where once again they were working on the trench system but were also sending working parties up to the front line trenches. On 6 September they were relieved, and they returned to just outside Bouzincourt, where they bivouacked and got cleaned up after their duty in the muddy and waterlogged trenches.

For a large portion of September, Tolkien and the 11th Fusiliers were behind the front line at various locations – drilling, training (practice makes perfect), parading, being inspected and honing their battle skills.

On 25 September, Tolkien and the 11th Fusiliers set off to return to the front line. Part of the journey was on foot and for part of it they were travelling by motor bus. They reached Bouzincourt on 27 September and bivouacked overnight. That evening, they moved up to the front line and into trenches by Thiepval Wood.

The Battle of Thiepval had first started on 1 July 1916, when the 36th (Ulster) Division had attacked and entered the Schwaben Redoubt. They had held out for the day but were not reinforced or re-supplied, and were beaten back by a German counter-attack. The 36th Division suffered over 5,000 casualties on 1 July, around half their total strength.

The new battle for Thiepval Ridge started on 26 September and, by the time Tolkien and the 11th Fusiliers were at the front line, the village of

Sausage Valley, close to the village of La Boisselle on the Somme, was given its name by British soldiers because the Germans would fly sausage-shaped observation balloons at the top of it. The next valley was called Mash Valley. In the picture are the 36th Ulster Division and, behind the car with the canvas roof, can be seen the field kitchens, with their chimneys sticking up into the air.

A mark 1 British tank or land-ship at Thiepval in September 1916. The tank body was constructed from half-inch boiler plates that were held in place with rivets. The anti-grenade guard can be seen on the roof of the tank and at the rear is the wheeled steering tail; both of these features were only used on the mark 1 tank.

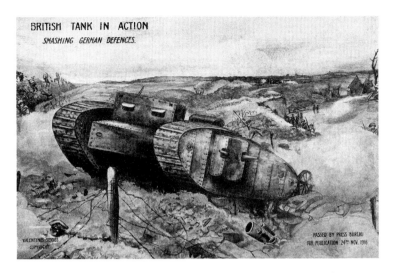

Tanks were first used in the third major offensive of the Battle of the Somme, on 15 September 1916, in the Battle of Flers-Courcelette.

A propaganda picture of a battle-scarred – but victorious – tank, mud-caked and slightly damaged, coming into Albert after battle on 15 September 1916. The tank had little success initially because of limited numbers, breakdowns and a lack of tank warfare skills.

Thiepval and a number of German trenches had been captured. The new wonder-weapon, the tank, had been used in the capture of Thiepval village, although it had first been used earlier in the month in the Battle of Flers-Courcelette. Tolkien slept in a German dugout in Thiepval on the night of 27 September.

On 28 September, Tolkien and the 11th Fusiliers were in the front line on the edge of Thiepval Wood; they had a grandstand view of the attack by the 18th Division on the Schwaben Redoubt. This attack was made using a method that was new for the British Army, where the troops advancing across no-man's-land were following a short distance behind a creeping artillery barrage. This would keep the German defenders down in their deep bunkers, and stop them from setting up their machine guns to mow the British troops down – as had happened on 1 July on the first day of the Battle of the Somme. Following an artillery barrage must have been a particularly scary thing to do, even on the Somme which was a place already brimming with death and destruction.

On the evening of 28 September, three patrols from the 11th Fusiliers attacked across no-man's-land and gained access through the German barbed-wire into a German trench in the salient known as the Pope's Nose. One can only wonder what a good Catholic lad like Tolkien thought of this name. They cleared the trench by throwing hand-grenades, and took a

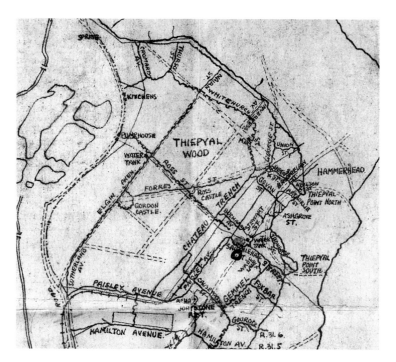

Trench Map – Thiepval Wood – Royal Engineers. Hand-drawn map, pre-1 July 1916. (Reproduced with kind permission of G.H. Smith & Son, Easingwold, York, printers and publishers of facsimile First World War trench maps, First World War Michelin Guides, First World War postcards and other First World War printed memorabilia. www.ghsmthbookshop.com)

Waves of British troops attacking the Schwaben Redoubt, a German fortification close to the village of Thiepval. It was named by the German 26th Division who were defending it, who came from Swabia, which is the common name for the south-western part of Germany. The Schwaben Redoubt was made up of three interconnected lines of trenches, tunnels and artillery emplacements, and was an anchor point in the German defence line on the Somme.

British troops capturing the summit of the Schwaben Redoubt on 28 September 1916. The Germans held the north face until 14 October 1916.

British troops capturing and clearing a German trench.

British troops destroying a German dugout in a shell-damaged trench.

number of German prisoners. Tolkien spoke to one of the wounded German officers in German, offering him a drink of water. The officer pulled Tolkien up on his German pronunciation, a strange thing to do in the middle of a battle.

On 30 September, Tolkien and the 11th Fusiliers were relieved from front line duty by the Royal West Kents, and marched back to the Bouzincourt area where they rested-up, trained and paraded for the next six days.

German prisoners being marched along a chalk roadway under guard – but it must be said that the scene looks quite relaxed.

A drawing of a ruined church in Ovillers in 1916.

On 6 October, with the autumn weather now taking hold and 1 July a distant dream, they returned to the front line, marching through Ovillers and passing by the shell-damaged ruins of a church and into the hinterland beyond Thiepval to the recently captured German positions at Mouquet Farm, sometimes called 'Mucky Farm' by the British troops.

Tolkien and the 11th Fusiliers moved into the captured trenches – called Zollern and Hessian Trenches by the Germans; they were relieving the 11th

The caption to this Realistic Travels stereo picture reads: 'After the assault on Mouquet Farm, Thiepval Ridge taken by our matchless infantry at heavy cost.' The picture was most likely posed for, as the losses in reality would have been much greater.

Cheshires and were facing German Marines in the Regina Trench. Battle was raging to their left, as Canadian troops fought to capture the remaining sections of the Schwaben Redoubt from the Germans. The Fusiliers were once again improving the trench system and Tolkien was most likely overseeing the installation of new, buried communication cables back to headquarters. The Germans were constantly shelling the trenches, and a number of men were killed or wounded.

Tolkien and the 11th Fusiliers moved out of the Hessian Trench on 12 October, and on 13 October they moved into the trenches at the Zollern Redoubt, a short distance from the Hessian Trench; here they were shelled with tear gas.

They spent the next three days in the Zollern and Hessian Trenches working on the trench system, and Tolkien was involved with improving the communication systems. The final German-held section of the Schwaben Redoubt was captured on 14 October.

British troops under attack from German gas. Some soldiers are still putting on their gas masks and waiting for the strange and eerie sight of the German troops, also in their gas masks, advancing through the clouds to attack the British trench.

On 17 October, Tolkien and the 11th Fusiliers moved back to Ovillers. The British high command had put the German front line under the magnifying glass; they were planning their last moves before the winter weather set in. They were planning to attack and capture the German Regina Trench, which would give them the strategic high ground, overlooking the German positions on this section of the front line. Tolkien was given a map of the area, drawn up from aerial photographs and intelligence obtained from captured German prisoners.

On 18 October, the Fusiliers were issued with their orders and spent the day preparing for the battle to come. They set off for the front line at 10.30 p.m. and reached the Hessian Trench in the early hours of the following morning. Due to heavy rainfall and the area consequently turning into a sea of mud, the attack planned for that day was delayed for two days. On 20 October, Tolkien and the 11th Fusiliers were back in Ovillers; here they were issued with stores for the forthcoming battle and moved back up to the Hessian

A German trench system photographed from 8,000ft. The front line trenches can be seen zig-zagging backwards and forwards; this method of construction was to stop shell blasts or gunfire going straight along the trench.

German prisoners in a temporary compound – or 'in the bag' – with a large crowd of British troops looking on. The doorways at the rear of the picture most likely led to dugouts for the troops to sleep in – a sort of Hobbit hole, it could be said!

Trench, now referred to as the 'Lancs Trench'. All were in position by 3 a.m. on 21 October. The sunrise that morning brought a clear and frosty view across the few hundred metres to the Regina Trench. During the night, the Fusiliers had prepared their exit point for the impending attack. Tolkien, with his signals team, equipment and runners, was in a dugout in the front line trenches.

The attack started just after midday with an artillery barrage. The Fusiliers left the Hessian Trench, crossing no-man's-land behind a creeping barrage, finally falling on the Regina Trench. The attack was a great success and the Germans were caught off-guard. At 12.20 p.m., Tolkien signalled to headquarters that the Hessian Trench was receiving German prisoners. As the afternoon progressed, news filtered through that other sections of the Regina Trench had been captured. The 11th Fusiliers had linked up with the units on each side of them and had taken over 700 German prisoners; many more lay dead in the Regina Trench. The 11th Fusiliers had fifteen men killed, twenty-six reported missing and 117 wounded.

13

Trench Fever

olkien and the Fusiliers were taken out of the front line on Sunday 22 October. As they moved back, shells exploded around them. On their way to Ovillers they encountered a number of the new wonder-weapons – tanks grinding their way slowly up to the front line. They moved into a tented camp outside Albert and took part in a number of parades and inspections, then moved to a hutted camp before going on a route march to Beauval. Tolkien had been at around fifty different locations since arriving in France in June. Now relatively safe behind the front line, he was starting to feel unwell and, on 27 October, he reported sick to the medical officer with a high temperature; Tolkien was coming down with trench fever.

Trench fever, or, as it was sometimes called, 'five day fever', was first noticed on the Western Front in 1915, although it may have occurred before then. The first actual article about it was written in September 1915 by Major J. Graham, and was called 'A Note on a Relapsing Febrile

British stretcher-bearers carrying a sick or wounded soldier back to a field dressing station.

The small French town of Beauval was around 12 miles behind the front lines. Tolkien was billeted here in late October 1916 and it was here that he came down with trench fever.

'Illness of Unknown Origin'. The first time it was called 'trench fever' was in a publication by Captain G.H. Hunt and Major A.C. Rankin in October 1915.

Trench fever was once described as 'a disease of squalor' and was caused and spread by body lice, sometimes called 'chats' (*pediculus corporis*). The disease was caused by a bacterium called Bartonella Quintana (older names were Rochalimea Quintana and Rickettsia Quintana) which lived in the stomach wall of the louse. Another route for infection was troops scratching their skin – any louse excreta on their skin could remain infectious for several weeks.

The lice could move from soldier to soldier in the sometimes closely packed trenches, and could only survive for a few days away from human contact. One night, when Tolkien was in a German dugout, he and his colleagues bedded down and masses of hungry lice attacked them. The lice had lost their German hosts, who had been killed, captured or had withdrawn from the dugout. Naphthalene, in the form of a powder or paste, was used to stop inundations of lice; a concoction was made from naphthalene, creosote and iodoform, known as 'NCI'. Tolkien was given some ointment when he was in the German dugout, but claimed that it encouraged the lice.

The lice lived in the seams and folds in the soldiers' uniforms. The best way to destroy them was by washing the uniforms in very hot water and taking hot baths, but this was not practical in the trenches. However, the troops had their own method of removing the lice from their clothing – this was know as 'chatting up' and is where the verb 'chat' comes from, as the troops would undertake this task in groups and make it a social event. The method used to remove the lice was to hand-pick them off the clothing, or to run the flame of a candle up and down the seams or folds – but this was only a short-term cure as more lice would be back after a brief time.

Trench fever took between eight and thirty days to incubate in its victims and, with the onset of the disease, which came on suddenly, the patient suffered severe headaches, muscle pains in the trunk and legs, shivering attacks, and in some cases a pink rash that only lasted a short time. These symptoms were sometimes confused with the symptoms of influenza. Commonly, the fever only lasted for five days – hence the name 'five day fever' – but in some cases it recurred again and again, and victims were unfit for duty for up to three months. Trench fever was not fatal in most cases, but men often suffered from attacks of depression after recovering from the illness. Around 800,000 cases of trench fever were recorded during the war. Strangely, trench fever had almost completely disappeared after the Armistice in November 1918. However, this disease was to be upstaged by a greater epidemic later in the war – influenza.

WARD CAR
Continental Ambulance Train–
Built at G.W.R Works, Swindon.1915.

The inside of an ambulance carriage on an ambulance train, with hinged bunks for the wounded and sick troops; the top bunks must have been for the walking wounded. There were around forty bunks per carriage.

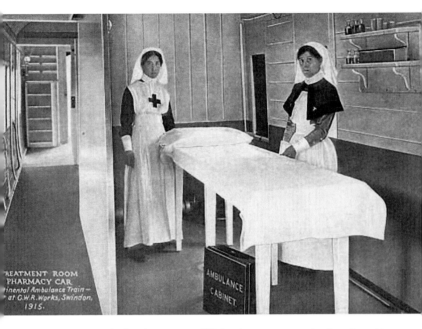

The treatment room in the pharmacy car. This is where emergency treatment would have been given to the troops en route to hospital.

Owing to his trench fever, Tolkien was admitted to an officers' hospital at Gezaincourt on 28 October. The next day he was taken by ambulance train to Le Touquet on the French coast.

In Le Touquet, Tolkien was admitted to the Duchess of Westminster's Hospital for officers, which was in a converted casino on the seafront. The fever raged on for a further nine days and would not die down, so Tolkien was taken again by train to Le Havre and put on the hospital ship HMHS *Asturias*, bound for Southampton on the south coast of England.

HMHS *Asturias* offloaded her cargo of sick and wounded soldiers at Southampton Docks, and Tolkien was put on a hospital train bound for his old hometown of Birmingham. He would have arrived at Selly Oak railway station in Birmingham, most likely at night, and been transferred to a two-wheeled ambulance trailer that was towed by a civilian car. The trailers were designed by a local man, a Mr E. Tailby, and were pretty claustrophobic inside, but the journey was only a short one through Selly Oak to the First Southern Military Hospital. This was in the University of Birmingham, which had opened in 1909 and was designed to be turned into a military hospital in times of war. By 1916 it had 1,570 beds. Many of the schools and grand houses close to other railway stations in the

area had become annexes of the hospital, to cope with the ever-increasing flood of casualties from the war.

So, Tolkien was back home in Birmingham, the place of his boyhood and the early days of his romance with Edith. He was not in a hut, tent, dugout, trench or farm building, but in a nice comfortable bed and being nursed by the Royal Army Medical Corps (RAMC), Red Cross nurses and St John Ambulance volunteers. One of the surgeons was Major Leonard Gamgee – Gamgee was a name from Tolkien's past and also his future. He had first come across the name while living in Stirling Road after his mother Mabel's death – the widow of Sampson Gamgee, father of Leonard, was living over the road from Tolkien. Sampson had invented 'Gamgee-tissue' – used to dress wounds and much in use at the time – and Tolkien was to use the name Sam Gamgee for Frodo's servant and friend in *The Lord of the Rings* many years later.

By early December, with good hospital nursing and, hopefully, good English cooking, Tolkien's temperature had returned to normal, but he was

Le Touquet seafront.

The inside of one of the
gaming rooms in a Le Touquet
casino. These rooms were
converted into hospital wards
by removing the furniture,
wrapping the chandeliers in
sheets and installing beds.
It became the Duchess of
Westminster's Hospital for
officers.

The view down Rue de Paris in Le Havre, where Tolkien was taken prior to leaving for England by hospital ship.

The docks at Le Havre, where Tolkien most likely boarded the hospital ship HMHS Asturias for the voyage across the English Channel to Southampton.

not 100 per cent fit still, with many aches and pains. Tolkien went before a military medical board and was given six weeks to convalesce before returning to duty.

Tolkien's school friend Geoffrey Smith, who was serving in France with the 19th Lancashire Fusiliers, was wounded by shrapnel on 29 November 1916. Although only a minor wound, he developed gas-gangrene, caused by soil-borne anaerobic bacteria. He died in the early hours of the morning on 3 December and is buried in Warlincourt Halte Cemetery in France.

I have often wondered if, during Tolkien's time in hospital, a seed for part of the character of Galadriel was planted in his mind. While suffering from trench fever, the RAMC nurses would have been a powerful image in his fevered mind, dressed in their white uniforms. The sisters would have

HMHS *Asturias* was built in 1907 for the Royal Mail Steam Co. and plied her trade between Southampton and Buenos Aires. When the war started in 1914 she was requisitioned by the Admiralty and converted into a hospital ship. She operated between France and Britain, bringing back wounded. She had accommodation for 896 patients, but on one trip she carried 2,400 wounded and sick servicemen from the Western Front. She was torpedoed by a German U-boat off the south coast of England on 20 March 1917 after unloading her cargo. Sadly, thirty-five of her crew and medical staff were killed. She survived the attack and became a floating ammunition store in Plymouth. After the war, she was rebuilt and renamed the *Arcadian*.

The Empress Dock, Southampton

Southampton docks, where HMHS *Asturias* would have docked with her cargo of sick and wounded troops from Northern France in 1916.

The nurses and orderlies who staffed a hospital train. Each nurse would have had around forty patients. The orderlies acted as stretcher-bearers, cooks and security staff – and what a smart and proud team they look in the picture.

Selly Oak railway station in South Birmingham, looking towards Bournville. Beyond the station the goods yard can be seen, where the hospital trains would unload the wounded and sick patients en route to the First Southern Military Hospital at the University of Birmingham. (Courtesy of Tom Hill)

Birmingham University was opened in 1909 and was designed to become a military hospital in times of war. It became the First Southern Military Hospital in 1914 and took its first wounded troops on 1 September 1914.

Birmingham University Great Hall, with 'Old Joe' clock tower behind it.
In the spring of 1915 the hospital had room for up to 1,000 beds, and in the summer of 1916 a further 570 beds were added. At its peak it had 130 officers and 2,357 other ranks as patients.

An interior view of the Great Hall at the University of Birmingham, serving as a huge hospital ward.

BIRMINGHAM UNIVERSITY AS A MILITARY HOSPITAL . THE SISTERS QUARTERS .

The Sisters' Quarters were in the female hall of residence on the University of Birmingham campus. The picture shows a group of sisters taking a break in the grounds of the hall in their starched, white uniforms. Three of the sisters are wearing their short shoulder capes.

Nurses taking tea in the grounds of a wartime hospital, looking very refined and relaxed. Most of the time the nurses would have been run off their feet, looking after the troops in their care.

A nurse raising funds for the Red Cross. This was not an uncommon sight at railway stations and in shopping centres during the war.

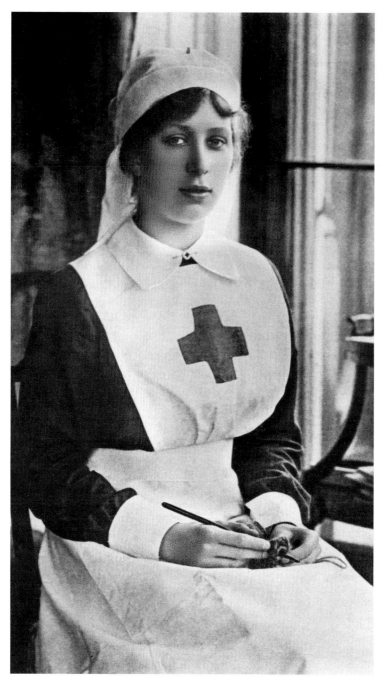

HRH Princess Mary was a Red Cross nurse during the First World War. This picture was taken at Buckingham Palace. During the war it was 'all hands to the pumps'.

The Lord watch between me and thee, when we are absent one from another.

Christmas, 1916.

To ....

From ....

One of the religious postcards sent at Christmas 1916 to the soldiers at the front. Many a wife, mother or sweetheart had already lost their husband, son, or lover in the Battle of the Somme and had no one to send cards like this to.

had to be strong and compassionate ladies to cope with the wounded – and sometimes delirious – troops they were treating. The image of a figure all in white moving from bed to bed could have emerged many years later when Tolkien was writing *The Lord of the Rings*.

> Very tall they were, and the lady no less tall than the Lord; and they were grave and beautiful. They were clad wholly in white.
>
> (*The Fellowship of the Ring*, The Mirror of Galadriel,
> J.R.R. Tolkien)

A hospital ward, possibly decorated for Empire Day, 24 May. The soldier, front right, has lost his foot.

14

After the Battle of the Somme

In early December, Tolkien took the train back to Great Haywood from Birmingham. At the time, the railways would have been heaving with troops, and congested with wartime goods traffic.

While Ronald had been away, Edith had plotted his locations in France from the coded information in his letters and marked them on the map she had on the wall of her lodgings. It could be said that by doing this she was playing with fire, as in the wrong hands this would be called spying.

British troops at a railway station during the war; most of the troops in the picture are cavalry. Some of the men are drinking tea and eating sandwiches. The boilers for heating the water for the tea can be seen on the left of the picture.

Great Haywood railway station. This would have been an important link to the outside world for both Ronald and Edith Tolkien while they were living in Great Haywood. It would also have been very busy, with troops coming and going from the camps on Cannock Chase.

Tolkien would have dreamt about getting back to Great Haywood while he was in France and in hospital, desperate to be with his wife Edith who he had not seen for over five months. Images of the places in and around Great Haywood – like the Rivers Trent and Sow, joining just above Essex Bridge – emerge in Tolkien's poem 'The Grey Bridge of Tavrobel', a romantic tale of love and desire. But war was never far away, even in Great Haywood; there were soldiers coming and going in the village, the sound of rifle fire from the ranges on the Chase blew in on the wind, and memories of fighting in the trenches must have played on Tolkien's mind.

War can be a strange thing – short periods of adrenaline-packed action with death and destruction all around, and long periods of boredom either in camp or waiting in the reserve or the line before going into action. Tolkien had churned thoughts and images over and over in his mind and, on his return to Great Haywood, words were leaking from his fingers, so he started to write what was to become *The Book of Lost Tales*; this was not published in his lifetime. Within *The Book of Lost Tales* are the major themes that were to become the basis of *The Silmarillion*, a book he worked on for most of the rest of his life, which was also not published in his lifetime.

In the second week of January 1917 he had returned to Birmingham, and should have been fit and ready for duty. However, he was still unwell, having had a further two outbreaks of trench fever (although neither as severe as his first attack). On 23 January he was back before the military medical board at the First Southern Military Hospital and they decided that he needed more time to convalesce, so he went back to Great Haywood and Edith for another month. On 23 February he returned to Birmingham and, at the end of February, he was examined by another military board in Lichfield. He was found to be still unfit for service but was assigned to the 3rd Lancashire Fusiliers on his return to fitness. Meanwhile, he was sent to a convalescent hospital for officers in Furness, Harrogate, in Yorkshire.

On 19 April, Tolkien returned to duty with the 3rd Lancashire Fusiliers at Thirtle Bridge Camp, near Withernsea, on the shore of the North Sea, just above the mouth of the Humber River. The Fusiliers were defending the north shore of the Humber River from invasion by the Germans; they were also training new recruits to the army. By this time, some of the new recruits were most likely conscripted men (conscription had been introduced in January 1916 as the flow of volunteers had virtually dried up due to the attrition of men on the Western Front).

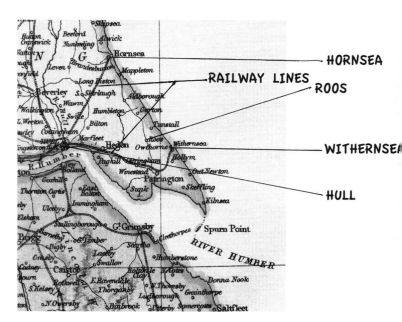

The mouth of the Humber River. Hornsea and Withernsea can be reached by train via Hull.

Edith had moved away from Great Haywood to be close to Ronald and, by this time, she was pregnant with their first child. She and her cousin Jennie moved into furnished rooms in Hornsea, some 20 miles further up the coast. Jennie must have been a pillar of strength and much-needed company for Edith at this time, considering all the things that Ronald had gone through during his period of war service and illness.

Later in the spring, Tolkien was put in charge of a coastal defence unit just outside Thirtle Bridge Camp in the village of Roos, where it is said that he had accommodation next to or close to the village post office. Edith moved in with him and the couple took walks in the area when Ronald was off duty. On one such walk they came across a wood – local tales allege it to be Dents Garth, the wood beside All Saints' Church.

Edith sang and danced for Ronald on the woodland floor, which was covered in spring flowers (described by Tolkien as hemlock). From this

All Saints' Church, Roos. Next to the church stands Dents Garth Wood, where it is said that Edith danced and sang for Ronald in the spring of 1917. The Avenue refers to the line of trees on each side of the path up to the church, and a kissing-gate can be seen to the right of the main gate.

interlude in the woodland, Tolkien wrote *The Tale of Beren and Lúthien*, in which Beren, a mortal man, falls in love with Lúthien, an immortal elven-maid. This became the central theme of *The Silmarillion*. Tolkien considered himself to be Beren and Edith to be Lúthien; these names are recorded on their gravestone in Wolvercote Cemetery in Oxford.

In 1968, Ronald and Edith left Oxford and moved to a bungalow on Lakeside Road in Poole, Dorset and spent three happy years living there till Edith's death in 1971. The bungalow has now been demolished and the two houses that have replaced it are called Lúthien and Beren. Although their home has gone from the site, the memory of Ronald and Edith will still live on there.

In early June 1917, Tolkien was examined by a military medical board in Hull and was found fit for military duty. But, in August, he had a fever again and was admitted to Brooklands Hospital for officers in Hull. During his stay in hospital, he may have heard the bomb explosions caused by Zeppelins around the Humber.

In late September, Edith and Jennie moved back to Cheltenham. Edith, by this time, was heavily pregnant and was to remain there till the birth of her first child. In mid-October, after nine weeks in hospital, Tolkien was still not fully recovered but was considered fit for home duties and returned to the 3rd Lancashire Fusiliers. In mid-November, Tolkien was medically examined again but was still unfit for overseas service.

On 16 November Edith gave birth to their first son, John, after a difficult and life-threatening labour. Ronald could not get leave for almost a week to go and visit them in Cheltenham. He sold the last of his mother's shares in South African mining to pay for Edith's medical care. Edith returned to Roos in Yorkshire and moved into furnished rooms. Tolkien was promoted to a full lieutenant, and once again this was announced in *The Times*, on 26 November.

Tolkien was still serving in Yorkshire but was now in the Home Service Garrison Battalion. In the first few months of 1918 he was examined by the medical board on several occasions but was still considered unfit for overseas duty. He also suffered an attack of influenza and was bedridden for five days with it.

Tolkien could have had what, at the time, was called 'three-day fever' – later called the Spanish Flu even though the Spanish called it the French Flu. This epidemic was to sweep around the world in 1918/19 three times, and may have killed over 70,000,000 people worldwide. It most likely had a hand in bringing the war to an end, as troops on both sides of the front line were infected by the virus. There is a strong body of evidence that the outbreak started in France at the Étaples camps in December 1916.

A postcard sent after the Armistice in 1918 by an unknown Australian soldier, who has had the flu and survived and is looking forward to going home.

There, far more troops were dying in the hospitals from sickness than from wounds, and the overcrowded conditions in the camps and trenches were breeding grounds for influenza.

At the time, this flu-like disease was called purulent bronchitis, and one of the first known victims was a soldier called Harry Underdown, who died in February 1917 and is buried at the military cemetery at Étaples.

Most flu viruses have their origins in birds, but sometimes these viruses can jump from one species to another. In 1916, chickens, geese and pigs were being kept at the Étaples camps – pigs can be a very good mixing bowl for these types of virus. Many soldiers had damaged lungs from poison-gas attacks, and these weakened organs were also fertile breeding grounds for the flu virus. The virus was carried all over the world by troops and people travelling on trains and boats, becoming a worldwide pandemic in 1918. Tolkien was lucky that he was not taken to a hospital in Étaples in October 1916 when he came down with trench fever.

On 10 April, Tolkien was passed fit for general military service by the medical board at the Humber Garrison headquarters, and was later posted back to Rugeley Camp and billeted in the Penkridge Bank section of the camp on Cannock Chase (where he first trained in 1915). Edith, their son John and cousin Jennie moved to Gypsy Green on the Teddesley Estate, an isolated hamlet close to the town of Penkridge, near the camps on Cannock Chase. Tolkien cycled to Gypsy Green to spend time with Edith and John when he was not on duty at the camp, and recorded the place in many drawings he did on his visits – in the same way that we would take photographs today to record our lives. Tolkien had been writing poetry throughout the war years; maybe he thought it safer to work on short stanzas of poetry rather than on a book, given that death could be just around the corner. But here at Gypsy Green he was once again turning his mind to *The Book of Lost Tales*, a much larger project than his poetry.

In the June of 1918, Tolkien moved across the Chase to Brocton Camp and, at the end of the month, he was once again stricken by illness in the form of gastritis, inflammation of the stomach lining. Although there was a hospital at Brocton Camp, Tolkien was moved across the country to the east coast, possibly once again to the Brooklands Hospital for officers in Hull.

Edith decided to stay in Gypsy Green and not follow Ronald to Hull. Since their marriage in 1916, Edith and Jennie had moved around England more than twenty times, following Ronald on his odyssey of camps and hospitals. Edith was still weak from giving birth to John and had her hands full caring for him. Maybe the place name, Gypsy Green, where she was living, was the straw that broke the camel's back and focused her mind on staying in one place for a while.

During Tolkien's stay in hospital in July and August he had become a shadow of his former self, having lost a great deal of weight. On 26 July, Tolkien was issued with orders to rejoin his battalion in France. The orders were rapidly rescinded as he was still in hospital and his battalion had been wiped out close to the River Aisne in France in May 1918. In September, Tolkien moved from the east coast of England to the west coast, to the Savoy Convalescent Hospital in the seaside resort of Blackpool. In the October of 1918, Tolkien was discharged from the hospital in Blackpool. He was now considered unfit for military service and for a time was on leave. By the end of the month he had returned to Oxford.

Tolkien was looking for work. He contacted William Craigie, who had taught him Icelandic and at the time was working on the New English Dictionary. William offered him a job working on the dictionary. Ronald became an assistant lexicographer of the dictionary, working on the W section, and it's nice to think that when you look up a word starting with W you are using some of Tolkien's early printed work. The work was being undertaken in the Old Ashmolean Building on Broad Street, next door to Exeter College.

The war finished on 11 November 1918, when the Armistice was signed by the Germans and the Allies; the sense of relief for the survivors of the war must have been incredible – they had survived! Tolkien contacted army authorities to seek permission to stay in Oxford until his demobilisation.

A view of the camps on Cannock Chase during the First World War.

The sign at the end of the private track leading to Gypsy Green on the Teddesley Estate.

Tolkien was joined in Oxford, just before Christmas 1918, by Edith, John and Jennie. They had rooms in St John Street, Oxford. Tolkien had finally returned to the street in Oxford where he had had rooms while still at Exeter College, just after the start of the war; but he had returned with a wife and child and memories of war, death, comradeship, illness and the raw courage of the men who had fought with him and died in the trenches.

Of Tolkien's direct peer group from school and college, 243 former schoolboys from King Edward's School were dead and 141 former students from Exeter College were dead. But this was a common tale for all survivors of the war.

15

War Memorials

irtually every village, town and city in Great Britain has got memorials to the dead from the First World War; France and Belgium also have memorials, and cemeteries large and small spread across the battlefields of the First World War. They record the dead from many far-flung corners of the world, as this was a war of world empires, mainly fought on land in northern Europe by the British and French Empires, and later by the United States, against the German Empire. Many men and some women have no known graves, and are still out there in no-man's-land in the now long-forgotten trenches. However, their

The Thiepval Memorial is located in Northern France, Picardy, near to the village of Thiepval. It records the names of 72,195 missing British and Commonwealth men who died in the Somme battlefields between July 1915 and February 1918. It is the biggest battle memorial in the world, standing 150ft high. When the remains of a soldier listed on the memorial are found and identified, the remains are buried with full military honours in the nearest cemetery to the find location and the name is removed from the Thiepval Memorial. The monument stands close to the trenches where Tolkien and the 11th Fusiliers fought in late September 1916. (Courtesy of Terry Carter)

Portland stone panels recording the names of the missing British and Commonwealth men on the Thiepval Memorial. (Courtesy of Terry Carter)

names are recorded in stone on cemetery walls and on monuments to the First World War. Shown in this chapter are some large and small memorials, but all are equally important to the relatives of the dead from the Battle of the Somme. There is even one that Tolkien would have seen and cycled past when he lived in Oxford.

> 'At the going down of the sun and in the morning,
> we will remember them.'

Ulster Memorial, Thiepval

The Ulster Memorial at Thiepval was 'unveiled' on 19 November 1921 by Field Marshal Sir Henry Wilson. It is a close copy of Helen's Tower in County Down, where many of the men of the 36th (Ulster) Division trained before going to France in 1916. The tower is a memorial to the more than 5,000 casualties of the 36th Division that attacked the heavily defended German position known as the Schwaben Redoubt on 1 July 1916. It stands close to the Thiepval Memorial.

The caribou sculpture in the Newfoundland Memorial Park, near Beaumont-Hamel on the Somme battlefield. The memorial park is in memory of the tragic events of 1 July 1916, and honours the Royal Newfoundland Regiment and Newfoundlanders who fought in the First World War – especially those with no known grave – and military personnel from both sides of the conflict. The park was opened by Field Marshal Haig in June 1925.

The Oxford War Memorial.

The Oxford War Memorial stands at the point where the Banbury Road and Woodstock Road join St Giles. There are no names recorded on it. Tolkien would have cycled past it on his way between Northmoor Road and his colleges after he returned to Oxford in 1925.

Bibliography

Allison, William and John Fairley, *The Monocled Mutineer* (Quartet Books, 1978)

Anonymous, *Alden's Oxford Guide* (Alden & Company Ltd, 1928)

Brown, Martin and Richard Osgood, *Digging Up Plugstreet* (Haynes Publishing, 2009)

Carpenter, Humphrey, *J.R.R. Tolkien: A Biography* (Unwin Paperbacks, 1978)

Carpenter, Humphrey, with the assistance of Christopher Tolkien (Eds), *The Letters of J.R.R. Tolkien* (Unwin Paperbacks, 1990)

Carter, Terry, *Birmingham Pals* (Pen & Sword, 1997)

Foster, Robert, *The Complete Guide to Middle-Earth* (Unwin Paperbacks, 1978)

Gardner, Angela and Jef Murray (Eds), *Black & White Ogre Country: The Lost Tales of Hilary Tolkien* (ADC Publications Ltd, 2009)

Garth, John, *Tolkien and the Great War* (Harper Collins Publishers, 2004)

Harris, John, *The Somme: Death of a Generation* (Zenith Books, 1966)

Morton, Andrew H. and John Hayes, *Tolkien's Gedling* (Brewin Books, 2008)

Norman, Terry, *The Hell They Called High Wood* (Patrick Stephens Ltd, 1984)

Scull, Christina and Wayne G. Hammond, *The J.R.R. Tolkien Companion and Guide* (Harper Collins Publishers, 2006)

Stedman, Michael, *La Boisselle: Somme* (Pen & Sword Military, 1997)

Stedman, Michael, *Thiepval: Somme* (Pen & Sword Military, 2005)

Tolkien, John & Priscilla, *The Tolkien Family Album* (Harper Collins Publishers, 1992)

Tolkien, J.R.R., *The Book of Lost Tales 1* (George Allen and Unwin, London, 1983)

Tolkien, J.R.R., *The Hobbit* (Unwin Books, 1967)

Tolkien, J.R.R., *The Lord of the Rings* (George Allen & Unwin Ltd, 1968)

Whitehouse, C.J. and G.P., *A Town for Four Winters* (Published by C.J. and G.P. Whitehouse, 1987)

Wilson, H.W. and J.A. Hammerton, *The Great War: The Standard History of the All Europe Conflict*, Volumes 1-10 (The Amalgamated Press Ltd, 1914-18)

The Battle of the Somme: DVD (The Imperial War Museum)

Index